D0033427

LITERARY
ST. PETERSBURG

✦

ELAINE BLAIR

LITERARY ST. PETERSBURG

A GUIDE TO THE CITY AND ITS WRITERS

THE LITTLE BOOKROOM
NEW YORK

Design: Louise Fili Ltd

Cover: View of the Neva and the Admiralteyskaya Embankment by
Moonlight, 1882, by Aleksandr Karlovich Beggrov. State Russian
Museum, St. Petersburg, Russia/The Bridgeman Art Library

Printed in China

Library of Congress Cataloging-in-Publication Data

Blair, Elaine.
Literary St. Petersburg: a guide to the city and its writers /
by Elaine Blair.
p. cm.
ISBN-13: 978-1-892145-37-6 (alk. paper)
ISBN-10: 1-892145-37-5 (alk. paper)
1. Literary landmarks--Russia (Federation)—Saint Petersburg.
2. Authors, Russian--Russia (Federation)—Saint Petersburg—
Biography.
3. Russian literature—Russia (Federation)—Saint Petersburg—
History and criticism.
4. Saint Petersburg (Russia)—Intellectual life. I. Title.
PG3505.L4B57 2007
891.709'94721—dc22   2006024950

Published by The Little Bookroom
1755 Broadway, 5th floor, New York, NY 10019
(212) 293-1643 Fax (212) 333-5374
editorial@littlebookroom.com
www.littlebookroom.com

Distributed by Random House and in the UK and Ireland by
Signature Book Services

CONTENTS

INTRODUCTION

*R*USSIAN LITERATURE BEGAN IN ST. PETERSBURG—A LATE START, CONSIDering that the city was founded in 1703. Russia was largely isolated from the West during the years of the Renaissance, and at the turn of the eighteenth century it was still feudal and deeply religious; the living conditions and world view of its people had changed little since medieval times. Even the nobility was largely uneducated. Secular art did not exist. Written Russian was used mainly for ecclesiastical writings and had little in common with the language that people actually spoke. When Milton was writing *Paradise Lost* and Molière his great plays, Russia still had no literary language to speak of.

But in 1682, Peter I, better known as Peter the Great, was crowned emperor. Within thirty years he had built a new city on Russia's western border, made it his capital, and set about transforming Russian society with ideas he had picked up in Germany, France, Holland, and Italy. It was his initial reforms of the Russian language, and his encouragement of a secular press, that allowed Russians to develop, over the course of the eighteenth and early nineteenth centuries, a literary language and a body of literature that was as rich, subtle, and expressive as anything in the West. The speed with which Russian literature "caught up" was extraordinary. The setting for this achievement was mainly St. Petersburg, where the first literary salons formed and the first of the famous "thick journals" on politics and literature were published.

Russian literature, however, has not always shown gratitude to the city that nurtured it. Anyone who has read *Crime and Punishment* or *War and Peace* knows that Dostoevsky and Tolstoy don't have much good to say about the city, and indeed Russia's best writers have as often maligned Petersburg as celebrated it. There are two ideas about the city that compete in the Russian imagination. On the one hand, it's Russia's most cosmopolitan city, with a history of tolerance, moderation, intellectual curiosity, and great achievement in the arts. Russia's first academies of science and art opened in St. Petersburg. The city's main avenue, Nevsky Prospect, is lined with "foreign" churches—Lutheran,

Peter the Great, 1772

Catholic, and Armenian—a testament to Petersburg's religious and national diversity in tsarist times. The system of rank established by Peter the Great allowed for greater social mobility than had been possible under the Moscow government. Dozens of new schools opened, including one where the children of servants could study Latin and Greek. As Peter hoped, his city became the entry point for ideas from the West, including political and artistic movements that transformed Russian society.

But from another point of view, Petersburg was, for two hundred years, the least free city in the country. Daily life was dominated by rigid social conventions imported from the West. The city's residents were closely watched by the tsar and his secret police. The streets were full of men in uniform, many of whom were trapped in the lower ranks of the civil service and returned home at night to apartments in Petersburg's unpicturesque slums. And even the wide avenues and monumental buildings of the city center seemed to some people sterile and intimidating, the proportions all wrong from the perspective of a person walking in the street. This oppressive Petersburg—"the most abstract and premeditated city in the world," in Dostoevsky's words—is one that we often see in nineteenth-century Russian novels and stories.

Petersburg's sinister reputation goes back to the peculiar circumstances of its founding. Peter the Great imposed his reforms on a deeply religious and superstitious public unused to change. To many of them, everything about Petersburg seemed strange, suspicious, and possibly blasphemous, beginning with the city's creation—at a record pace—on the site of what seemed to be a barely inhabitable swamp. Its wide avenues and baroque architecture were wholly unfamiliar in a country of small wooden houses, narrow alleyways, and onion-domed churches. Its residents were odd-looking too: Peter forced men to shave their beards and exchange long, loose robes for stockings and knee breeches. He encouraged his courtiers to learn French and other Western languages, and he recruited actual Westerners to come work in the city as architects, officers, bureaucrats, professors, tutors, and nannies. In Moscow, foreigners had been forced to live in the "German quarter," a neighborhood where they were segregated from Russians, who generally avoided them. But in Petersburg foreigners lived among Russians and mixed with them socially. Before Peter, the tsar had been thought to be divine. Peter, however, created secular institutions and insisted that religion no longer had a role in affairs of state. All these changes he enforced with strict oversight and threats of violence and imprisonment. He even went to social gatherings to make sure that the gentry was following his rules of decorum, which specified to the finest details how people should behave ("one must bow when others enter and leave").

The new capital and its residents were so different from the old that many Russians looked on the city with superstitious dread—surely Peter couldn't get away with all this. Stories spread that the city was haunted, that hundreds of thousands of workers had died while building it (many did die, but not an unusual number in an era of generally horrible working conditions), and that Peter's unloved first wife had put a curse on his city, saying that it would "stand empty." For years the city's destruction was thought to be imminent, an idea fueled by the fact that Petersburg was prone to catastrophic floods: in the eighteenth century the water would rise so high that some of the city's islands were completely submerged.

The ghost stories of a cursed city reemerged more than a hundred years later in the work of Alexander Pushkin, Nikolai Gogol, and Fyodor Dostoevsky, but by then they were inflected with political or social criticism. Russia's writers had a uniquely powerful role in the country's public life. Because of the tsar's absolute power, literature was one of the few arenas in which one could honestly assess the condition of the country or put forward a view of the world that differed from that of the tsar's (and, later, from that of the official Communist Party position). Writers were not only storytellers, but also spokesmen, agitators, and political symbols—in short, the conscience of their country. Not that they were completely free to speak their minds, for writing honestly was always risky, and almost all the writers in this book had some confrontation with the government, whether they were denounced, harassed, jailed, exiled, executed, or merely censored. Tsars paid extraordinarily close attention to what the writers were up to. Nicholas I, for example, intercepted and read Pushkin's letters. Petersburg was so closely associated with the tsar, his court, and his oppressive surveillance, that for some writers, portraying the city in a negative or ambivalent light was a way of obliquely criticizing either the regime or the state of Russian life.

The nineteenth century was a time of self-scrutiny among Russian intellectuals. Some wondered if Russia hadn't borrowed too much from the West after all. All over Europe there was a revival of interest in folk culture, but in Russia the nostalgia for simple country life was acute because well-born Russians were brought up reading foreign literature, speaking foreign languages, and learning Western traditions. While Slavophiles, as they were called, lamented Western influence on Russian life, other writers argued that Peter's reforms hadn't gone far enough. Russia was still ruled by autocrats who exiled or executed political dissidents, most of the population was virtually enslaved through serfdom, and even people who weren't serfs had far fewer rights under the law than did their Western counterparts.

No matter which side you were on, Petersburg could seem to symbolize everything that was wrong with Russia. Its social atmosphere, still noticeably different from that of the interior of the country, was simply too foreign and unspontaneous for some. For others its modern, Western appearance was painfully at odds with the despotic regime that governed there, which was beginning to seem distinctly non-Western as revolution and reform swept through the rest of Europe. Add to this the social problems faced by all industrializing cities—overcrowding, pollution, disease, crime— and you have a troubling, troublesome city.

And so Petersburg enters Russian literature as a problem—beautiful, to be sure, but overrefined, corrupt, oppressive, the symbol of everything that was wrong with Russian society. And as always its damp, mercurial weather came to the aid of those who wished to suggest that the city was doomed: the Petersburg of Pushkin, Gogol, Dostoevsky, and Alexander Blok is devastated by flood, flattened by fearsome wind, shrouded in fog, or battered by snowstorms. Even the lovely white nights, when the sun barely sets, could be made to seem creepy. Moscow, meanwhile, had developed a reputation as a much more convivial town: without constant surveillance by the tsar and his guards, people could speak and write more freely; social gatherings were less formal; and Muscovite noblemen, free from the obligations of the court, could spend their days hunting, restaurant-hopping, and entertaining into the night. It's no wonder that in Tolstoy's comparisons of the two cities, Petersburg does not fare well.

In spite of the beating it took in nineteenth-century novels, St. Petersburg continued to be a center of literary life through the turn of the century and the early years after the revolution, fertile periods for Russian literature when writers like Alexander Blok, Osip Mandelstam, Anna Akhmatova, and Vladimir Mayakovsky read their poems at late-night gatherings in private apartments and at the Stray Dog cabaret. Moscow emerged beside Petersburg as a second literary center, and there was much traveling back and forth among the bohemians. Boris Pasternak, Marina Tsvetayeva, and Andrei Bely, for instance, lived in Moscow but were regular visitors to Petersburg. Mayakovsky lived mostly in Moscow but followed his love, Lily Brik, and her husband to Petersburg in 1915, in time to witness the revolution first hand.

In these early years of the new century, ideas about Petersburg began to shift: an admiration for the city, and for the cosmopolitan spirit it represented, developed among the writers who lived there. The Westernized culture that Petersburg—soon to be Petrograd, then Leningrad—represented did not seem so foreign to Russians at the turn of the twentieth century as it had a hundred years before. Writers who came of age at the turn of the century or later—Vladimir Nabokov, Anna Akhmatova, Osip Mandelstam—did not see anything ominous in the city's beauty, even if they did see something ominous in its ineffectual last tsar and the revolutionaries who overthrew him. As the Soviets moved the capital back to Moscow in 1918 and revealed themselves to be the most brutal and xenophobic regime ever to rule Russia, Petersburg became a precious reminder of Russia's former Western ties and its once-lively intellectual life. Vladimir Lenin, Joseph Stalin, and Nikita Khrushchev were all afraid that the city's tradition of skeptical inquiry and its western location would make it a center of dissent, and they singled out Leningrad for special punishment with waves of arrests, executions, and imprisonment of its citizens. Between the chaos of the revolution, the purges of Stalin's Great Terror, and the German siege of the city in World War II (when the Nazis surrounded Petersburg and cut off supplies of food and fuel for nine hundred days), Petrograd-Leningrad suffered as no other European city did. Leningrad residents, most famously Akhmatova, described the horrors of the Terror and the blockade in memoirs and poetry and stories, but most of these works, like so much honest and original Russian writing, went unpublished until long after Stalin's death in 1953 (in some cases until the fall of the Soviet regime in the 1990s) while the writers were persecuted and killed. Nonsocialist writing went underground in the 1930s, distributed in secret or not at all, surfacing only occasionally in the sixties, seventies, and eighties.

Today Petersburg is half the size of Moscow, and it has not yet won back its old role as the literary and intellectual center of Russian life. Though there's a lively café scene of young artists and writers, most of the city's young people are struggling to get an economic foothold in the new Russia, and literary publishing itself has not fared particularly well in the new economy. Immediately after the fall of the Soviet Union there was an enormous appetite for the works of the serious authors who had been banned, but that appetite waned after a few years, and the print runs for books by Joseph Brodsky and Anna Akhmatova aren't what they used to be.

Over the decades Petersburg has been home to scores of novelists, poets, journalists, and essayists. In writing this book I've focused primarily on writers who not only lived in Petersburg but also wrote about the city. I've also included two writers, Leo Tolstoy and Andrei Bely, who did not live in the city for significant lengths of time but whose depiction of Petersburg has been particularly influential and inspired. I've limited this guide to writers whose work is easily available in English translation, though some will of course be less familiar to English readers than others. This is by no means an exhaustive list of Petersburg writers, or of the streets, monuments, and buildings that the writers described and inhabited. I've chosen the most significant and representative sites, which I hope will give a flavor of the city as well as of the writers, and I've assumed that most visitors to Petersburg will not want to ride two hours by subway, bus, and tram to see—for instance—the suburban park where Alexander Blok liked to take his afternoon walks. For readers who do want to learn and see more of literary Petersburg, there's a selected bibliography on page 133.

Alexander Pushkin, 1827

ALEXANDER PUSHKIN
1799–1837

RUSSIAN LITERATURE WAS STILL REL-ATIVELY NEW WHEN ALEXANDER Pushkin was born. Only a handful of poets, playwrights, and historians preceded him, and the literary language itself was still evolving. From a mix of colloquial Russian, French, and Church Slavonic (the ecclesiastical language of Russian Orthodoxy), Pushkin's eighteenth-century predecessors had shaped a modern literary Russian that awaited its first genius.

That genius was Pushkin, who was able to produce—before he died at thirty-seven—a collection of poetry and prose remarkable for its supple language, subtlety, liveliness, and wit. He wrote about aristocrats in St. Petersburg (a subject he knew from experience), as well as medieval Kievan princes, Moldovan gypsies, Crimean harem girls, Circassian tribes, and the sixteenth-century tsar Boris Godunov. He explained Russians to themselves, as a country and as individual souls, in a way no previous writer had. Many would argue that no subsequent writer has matched him. As is often the case with poetry, it's difficult to convey the particular qualities of Pushkin's writing in translation. (Vladimir Nabokov called his own translation of Pushkin's *Evgeni Onegin* "dove droppings on your monument.") When writers describe his poetry to non-

Emperor Alexander I reading a manifesto in St. Petersburg, 1861

Russian readers they usually compare him to another genius: Mozart. Like the composer, Pushkin had a way of making his art—which was unprecedented in its technical mastery—seem effortless, and his light touch would surprise readers who associate Russian literature with Dostoevsky and Tolstoy.

Pushkin spent most of his adult life in Petersburg. The "granite-clad Neva"—the river between its rock embankments—is a regular part of the landscape of his poems. He loved the beauty, and, for a time, the social life of the city—the balls, the gossip, the salons and card games and jockeying for rank. But Petersburg

social life was dominated by the tsar, who orchestrated or presided over most of the city's balls and entertainments, and Pushkin's relations with the court were never easy. Both Alexander I and his successor, Nicholas I, kept close watch over the writer. They read his poems, intercepted his letters, and were kept informed about private remarks that Pushkin made. Pushkin was no radical (he had the mildly liberal views typical of his generation of aristocrats), and he was not involved in political intrigue. In fact, he spent a good deal of effort trying to win back the favor of the tsars. But it was still unusual during Pushkin's lifetime for an aristocrat (much less a poorer man) to take up writing as his main occupation. Petersburg gentlemen were expected to be active members of the civil service or the military, driven by a code of ethics that valued service to the state above any other work. Pushkin's dedication to writing suggested a rare independence of mind that—combined with his irreverence and popularity—made him deeply suspicious to the court. In one way or another, the tsars and their cronies hounded Pushkin all of his life, and finally to his death.

Pushkin was born in Moscow in 1799 to rich parents from distinguished families. His father was the descendant of a very old family of Moscow gentry. On his mother's side, Pushkin was the great-grandson of Abram Gannibal, a black African who had been kidnapped into slavery as a boy but managed to become a prominent military engineer and join the ranks of the landed gentry in Russia. Neither of Pushkin's parents was very affectionate with their children, and like many upper-class Russian children of his generation he was raised mostly by a peasant nanny to whom he remained devoted his entire life. (She even lived with him during some of the years of his exile from Petersburg.) He went to boarding school at the fashionable new Imperial Lycée outside St. Petersburg. When he graduated he received a civil service position in the Foreign Office in Petersburg, though he seems never to have done much work there.

Instead he drank, played cards, had love affairs, and—when he could squeeze it in—wrote poetry. Pushkin's dissipation left him frequently ill with venereal diseases, and some of his most productive periods of writing came when he was bedridden. "Despite his whole dissolute way of life," one of his friends wrote, Pushkin "is finishing the fourth canto of his poem. If he were to have three or four more doses of clap, it would be in the bag."

His first major published work was a mock-heroic epic called *Ruslan and Lyudmila*, about a young bride in medieval Kiev who is kidnapped by a wizard the day of her wedding. The public loved *Ruslan and Lyudmila*, and Pushkin became famous. But fame could be dangerous for a Russian writer, for it drew the attention of the tsar. Soon after the poem was published Alexander I read some earlier stanzas that Pushkin had written about the cruelties of serfdom. At the time, many younger members of the nobility, including Pushkin's closest friends, were agitating for political reform. Threatened by the seditious mood in the capital, and worried that Pushkin's writing had too much influence over rebellious young people, Alexander banned Pushkin from Petersburg.

For the next six years Pushkin wandered through southern Russia, living for brief periods in the Caucasus, the Crimea, Kishinev, and Odessa. His time in the south was the inspiration for two much-loved narrative poems published in the early 1820s: *The Captive of the Caucasus* (about a Russian man in the Caucasus held prisoner by a Circassian tribe) and *The Fountain of Bakhchisaray* (about a Polish princess who is kidnapped into the harem of a Crimean khan). These poems mark the height of Pushkin's popularity in his own lifetime: he would gradually evolve a more austere style of poetry that readers found less dazzling, then move on to prose, which his contemporaries appreciated still less. Some of the works that we now consider masterpieces, including *Evgeni Onegin*, were greeted indifferently by the rising generation of readers at the time of their publication. The fervor with which Russians idolized Pushkin in the twentieth century has eclipsed the fact that he was considered a dinosaur in the last years of his life—a once-brilliant poet whose era had passed and whose talent had waned embarrassingly by the time he reached his thirties.

Tsar Nicholas I, 1826

Pushkin's exile finally ended in 1826, when the new tsar, Nicholas I, pardoned him and allowed him to live where he pleased. Pushkin promptly resumed his former pursuits—cards and women—but by now he had at least some faint inclinations toward family life. He proposed in 1829 to a beautiful teenager, Nat-alia Goncharova, whom he met at a ball in Moscow, and the couple soon settled in Petersburg. Pushkin adored her, but they were not a good match; she had little interest in poetry and lived for the capital's parties and balls, where she was a great success. Theirs was an expensive way of life, and the Pushkins acquired debts. To alleviate them, Pushkin had to curry favor at court, which he naturally found humiliating. Nicholas I personally combed through his writing and asked him to make changes, causing delays in publication and making his financial state all the more precarious. If Pushkin refused to bowdlerize his work the tsar would threaten to revoke his access to historical archives, making it impossible for him to work on a history of Peter the Great that he was writing. Most humiliating of all was that Natalia caught the eye of the tsar. So that he could flirt with her at palace events, Nicholas gave Pushkin the rank of "gentleman of the chamber," requiring him to attend all the balls—and bring his wife with him. The flirtation was innocent (though Natalia may have had an affair with the tsar later, after Pushkin's death). But Pushkin's calendar was filled with social events that he could hardly stand. He desperately wanted to get away to his country estate to write. The city became a prison.

In 1831, Pushkin made his last corrections to *Evgeni Onegin*, a "novel in verse" that he had been working on for eight years, about a bored Petersburg dandy and a country girl who falls in love with him.

He paints a sparkling picture of a young aristocrat's Petersburg, all theaters and balls and afternoon strolls of "total leisure" on Nevsky Prospect. Evgeni's story is narrated by an older, wiser friend of his who casts an amused eye at the young man's raucous romantic life. The narrator himself has outgrown such youthful amusements, and, unlike Evgeni, found a more rewarding pursuit in poetry.

Natalia Goncharova, 1820s

> I write…and want no more embraces;
> My straying pen no longer traces,
> Beneath a verse left incomplete,
> The shapes of ladies' heads and feet.

These were more or less Pushkin's own sentiments in his last years, when he longed for pen and paper and peace and quiet more than anything else. He turned to prose, completing a historical novel and several short stories, and began working on a bigger novel about contemporary life.

In the mid-1830s a young Frenchman, Georges d'Anthes, appeared in Nicholas's court and began to woo Natalia. She refused him, but the pair became the subject of gossip, and Pushkin received a mocking anonymous letter congratulating him on having joined the "Serene order of Cuckolds." He sent d'Anthes a angry note that he knew would lead to a duel. D'Anthes called Pushkin out. The story of their meeting one January afternoon on a snow-covered field is known by nearly every Russian. D'Anthes shot first, hitting Pushkin in the stomach. Pushkin fired back as he collapsed, but he only wounded d'Anthes. The poet was rushed home in a critical state and died from his bullet wound two days later. D'Anthes left for France and lived to a comfortable old age without ever expressing regret for having killed Russia's great poet.

Pushkin's most influential vision of Petersburg was the one he expressed in his last poem, *The Bronze Horseman*, which was published after his death. The poem is about a poor civil servant named Evgeni who dreams of a higher salary and a cozy domestic life with his fiancée. His dreams are ruined when a flood washes over Petersburg and kills his beloved. While wandering around the city heartbroken and half-mad, Evgeni stops at the equestrian statue of Peter the Great that sits in Senate Square (the bronze horseman of the title) and berates the tsar for having built the city on swampland, where floods are inevitable. The bronze Peter takes offense and pursues him through the city until the clerk collapses in exhaustion and dies at the threshold of the hut where his fiancée lived.

"Poor, poor Evgeni," as Pushkin calls him, prefigures the ordinary little men crushed by the city in Gogol and Dostoevsky's stories. And Peter the Great appears for the first time in Pushkin's work not simply as a national hero but also as a menace. The portrait was no doubt influenced by his own bitter experience with two of Peter's successors, an experience that itself seems to prefigure that of all the other Russian writers who would be watched, censored, and tormented by autocratic regimes.

PUSHKIN MEMORIAL FLAT
12 Naberezhnaya Moiki
(812) 311-3531
🚊 *Nevsky Prospect*
Daily 10:30 am–5 pm;
closed Tuesday and the last Friday of each month

Pushkin and his wife lived in six different Petersburg apartments between 1831—the year they were married—and his death in 1837. Their last apartment has been made into a museum. It's a suite of rooms in a larger mansion on the Moika River that belonged to the Volkonskys, an old noble family. The Pushkins and their four children moved into the apartment in September 1836. The rooms have been arranged more or less as they were in Pushkin's day. At that time apartments were rented already furnished; the Pushkins had few belongings of their own beyond Pushkin's many books. One of Pushkin's close friends, the poet Vasily Zhukovsky, sketched a plan of the apartment for posterity a few weeks after Pushkin died, and it was this sketch that the curators relied on when they re-created the flat and opened the museum in 1925.

The most arresting room in the museum is Pushkin's study, where he kept his library of roughly four thousand volumes in fourteen languages. The actual books on the shelves are reproductions, but his library is said to have included rare books, such as a 1596 edition of Dante's *Divine Comedy*. Visitors to the study can also see some specimens from Pushkin's walking stick collection, the oil lamp by which—his son claimed—he wrote *Evgeni Onegin*, and pages from his notebooks with drafts of poems and drawings. The study is where Pushkin lay after his duel with D'Anthes, and the clock in the room is set to 2:45 to mark the time of his death on January 29, 1837 (since Russia switched to the Gregorian calendar after the 1917 revolution the anniversary of Pushkin's death has been observed on February 10). Another room of the museum has Pushkin's death mask and a lock of his hair. The explanatory plaques are in Russian, but an English audio guide is available.

Vyborg Side

CHERNAYA RECHKA
Kolomyazhskiy Propsect
(at the intersection with Ulitsa Matrosa Zheleznyaka)
🚇 *Chernaya Rechka*

An obelisk in this small, scruffy park marks the spot where Pushkin was mortally wounded. When Pushkin met D'Anthes here in 1837 it was a quiet rural suburb of Petersburg. Today it's a semi-industrial, working-class neighborhood of high-rise apartments, auto body shops, and speeding traffic. Chernaya Rechka means "black stream" and refers to the local body of water, now uninvitingly oily and surrounded by concrete embankments.

Tsarskoe Selo

IMPERIAL LYCÉE AT TSARSKOE SELO
2 Sadovaya Ulitsa
(812) 476-6411
Minibuses: #K-286, #K-287, #K-299, or #K-342;
suburban trains to Tsarskoe Selo leave daily from
Vitebsk Station
Daily 10:30 am–4:30 pm; closed Tuesday and the last
Friday of each month

Most foreign tourists visit Tsarskoe Selo, just outside of Petersburg, to see the imperial palaces, but the town is also the site of Pushkin's lycée and of a dacha where he and his wife spent the summer of 1831 shortly after they were married. In fact, only the palace area is still called Tsarskoe Selo (meaning "royal village")—the town around the palaces is called Pushkin in honor of the poet. Pushkin loved going for long walks and sometimes would walk from Petersburg all the way to Tsarskoe Selo (about thirty kilometers) and back in one day.

The Imperial Lycée, where Pushkin studied from age twelve to sixteen, is now a museum (the Memorial Lycée-Museum, officially) in which visitors can see the main schoolroom, library, and bedrooms where the students slept, all of which are furnished as they were when Pushkin was a student from 1811 to 1817. The Imperial Lycée, the first lycée in Russia, opened in 1811—Pushkin was a member of its first class. It was meant to give the brightest sons of noble families a general education in languages (Russian, French, German, Latin), mathematics, history, rhetoric, and geography, as well as fencing, dancing, riding, and swimming. Boys began between the ages of ten and twelve and graduated six years later. One of the halls shows a chart with students' grades, including those of Pushkin, who was excellent at Russian, decent at Latin, and at the bottom of the class in math. On the top floor of the lycée is a long corridor with the boys' bedrooms. Pushkin's old room, number 16, is open to view. Though each boy had his own room, this didn't necessarily mean much privacy—the narrow rooms resemble stalls in a stable. For ventilation purposes the side walls don't go all the way to the ceiling, and the door to each room has a large window of wire mesh. It was while he was a student at the lycée that Pushkin began to write poetry—sometime in his fourteenth year—and to think of himself as a poet.

PUSHKIN DACHA MUSEUM

2 Pushkinskaya Ulitsa

(812) 312-1962

Minibuses: #K-286, #K-287, #K-299 or #K-342;

suburban trains to Tsarskoe Selo leave daily from

Vitebsk Station

Wednesday–Sunday 10 am–4:30 pm; closed Monday,

Tuesday, and the last Friday of each month

The Alexander Pushkin Country House Museum is a suite of rooms in a small house that Pushkin and his wife rented during the summer and early fall of 1831. The poet spent the mornings working and went for walks in Alexander Park in the evenings. He was already well known by then, and people would come to the park in hopes of catching sight of him on one of his walks. An engraving of the young Nikolai Gogol hangs in Pushkin's study. The poet was enthusiastic about Gogol's early work and invited the younger writer to visit him at the dacha that summer.

Nikolai Gogol

NIKOLAI GOGOL
1809–1852

THE FIVE SHORT STORIES THAT NIKO-
LAI GOGOL SET IN ST. PETERSBURG
changed the way that readers saw the city. Like the
haunted Petersburg of folk legends, Gogol's capital is
an inhospitable place not entirely subject to the laws of
nature, where the wind blows "from all four sides" at
once and the vast city squares look "like a terrible des-
ert, with houses barely visible on the other side." A city
dweller might be harassed by a ghost during an evening stroll, or find a nose in his slice of morning bread.
Any unexpected thing might happen in this city, Gogol
suggests, but most likely it will be something bad.

His Petersburg characters are clerks and young artists snubbed by pompous bosses and ignored by every-

one else. They live alone and have no family or friends to buffer their daily contact with the cruel social and professional hierarchies that dominate city life. Gogol was the first important Russian writer to write about the lives of the poor. For this he was embraced by liberal intellectuals and later generations of social reformers. But he couldn't have been further from a social reformer himself; he was deeply religious and conservative and would later infuriate his liberal admirers by suggesting that serfdom and autocratic rule were fine traditions that ought to be left alone. For much of his career, Gogol felt that he was misunderstood by readers. He depicted his characters' cruelty and humiliation and ineptitude in such specific detail that readers were sure was taking a stand against some particular institution (the civil service hierarchy, the provincial administration, serfdom) that in fact he had no quarrel with. He himself meant his stories to give moral instruction, but he had too wild an imagination for horrifying and pathetic and funny and not-strictly-relevant details to write simple parables. The ghost of Akaky Akakievich in "The Overcoat" might get his revenge on the pompous civil servant who tormented him, but the story doesn't end there—another ghost wanders in, and during the last few sentences of the story a whole new little episode unfolds, each detail more improbable than the next.

Gogol was born and grew up in Ukraine, in a family of devout small-time landowners. While still a gymnasium student he already imagined himself living in St. Petersburg, in a "cheerful little room" with windows overlooking the Neva. He had the vague hope of becoming famous there, though he wasn't sure for what. When he did move to the capital in 1828, at the age of nineteen, he had no money or social connections. Instead of a cheerful room overlooking the river, Gogol had to rent a series of dingy rooms in crowded boarding houses with shared kitchens, mostly in the modest neighborhoods around Gorokhovaya street and the Ekaterinsky Canal (now Griboedov Canal), the same places that his characters haunt. He was struck by the smell of alcohol concentrated in stairwells; the great variety of occupations that his neighbors pursued; and the poverty—both theirs and his own. As a student he had looked forward to attending St. Petersburg's great theaters, but now, he complained to his mother, he couldn't even afford the tickets.

When Gogol arrived in St. Petersburg the city was still in the shadow of the Decembrist uprising, in which protesters gathered on Senate Square in 1825 to demand a constitution from Nicholas I. The tsar ordered his troops to surround the demonstrators and fire on the crowd; more than one thousand people were killed, and several dozen of the organizers— who were mostly from the educated upper classes—were sentenced to exile, hard labor, or death. Afterward, intellectuals retreated from open political dissent, and aristocratic social life became orderly, at least on the surface.

During the first half of the nineteenth century the tsars expanded the state bureaucracy fivefold. The streets of the city were thick with men who had come from the provinces to work in the civil service, all wearing uniforms that reflected their precise rank and department. Gogol writes in his story "Nevsky Prospect" that at a certain hour in the afternoons it seemed that everyone on the streets was an employee of some ministry or other. "Suddenly spring comes to Nevsky Prospect: it gets all covered with clerks in green uniforms." The question of rank weighs heavily on the bureaucrats in Gogol's Petersburg stories. One clerk is so tormented by his lowly position that loses his mind and imagines he is the king of Spain.

Hoping to avoid such a fate, Gogol auditioned to be an actor at St. Petersburg's Bolshoi Theater (as a schoolboy he had been a devilishly good mimic), but he was unsuccessful. He borrowed money from his mother and self-published *Hans Küchelbaker*, a sentimental narrative poem about a German boy's coming of age— a subject and a style that didn't suit him, to say the least. The one literary critic who bothered to mention the book was unmerciful. Gogol and his servant (even relatively poor members of the gentry had a servant) bought every copy of the poem and burned them in a shabby hotel on the corner of the Ekaterinsky Canal and Vozenesensky Prospect. Still feeling wounded, he set off for America, but a week or so later he changed his mind and returned to the city—and got a job in the civil service.

In his spare time Gogol started writing stories about Ukrainian rural life. This was less a matter of personal interest than of expediency. There was a vogue for stories about Ukraine, and Gogol was well aware of this when he started writing about his home province, which had never interested him much when he actually lived there. In 1830 he had his first story published. His editor invited Gogol to a literary salon and introduced him to Pushkin, whom Gogol had passionately admired since his school days. Pushkin, for his part, praised Gogol's work—a heady honor for a young person—and introduced him to other writers.

Even before writing masterpieces like "The Overcoat" and *Dead Souls*, Gogol stood out in the small pool of Russian prose writers for his humor and his unusually expressive and complicated style, full of digressions and unexpected bursts of rhetoric, as well as brilliantly rendered colloquial Russian. His later work, however, also demonstrated something else: a brilliant imagination for many permutations of vice and vulgarity. In the mid-1830s he began writing the Petersburg tales and *The Government Inspector*, a play about a charlatan who makes a pile of money by convincing the politicians of a small provincial town that he is a government inspector come to check on their doings. The play was a huge success—it premiered at the Alexandrinsky Theater (p. 86) in 1836 and was performed another 272 times that year.

Gogol had finally become famous, but he was not entirely pleased with his success. He felt that his play had been misread by audiences as a satire of government corruption. As usual, he thought he was writing a parable: he had meant to indict Russian morals rather than Russian mores. At the same time, the play's enormous success made him conscious of his power over the public. If only he could succeed in writing the kind of grand religious work that he aspired to, he felt he would actually be able to direct Russia toward a new national destiny, an era of piety and fraternity. He would do this, he thought, by writing a huge novel. The first volume would introduce a rogue, who would then (in the second volume) see the error of his ways and (in the third volume) become pious and fraternal, showing the Russians how it's done. *Dead Souls* was published in 1842, but the second and third volumes never appeared: Gogol found it much easier to imagine the sins of his hero, Chichikov, than to imagine his repentance. The scenes of Christian heroes weren't any good, in his own eyes, compared to the huge cast of morally compromised provincial grotesques.

He spent the rest of his life, the next ten years, torn between his religious ideals and his artistic intuition before finally burning everything he had written and falling into despair. He refused food, became sick, and died in 1852. (In 1921, poet Alexander Blok (p. 61), another great Petersburg writer who was much influenced by Gogol's view of the city, would also starve himself out of despair and die of weakness and malnutrition.) After Gogol, it became fashionable for writers to find something menacing in the landscapes, weather, and street life of St. Petersburg. The idea of a haunted city lived on into the twentieth century, by which time the residents were suffering such horrors as to make all the writers' dark intimations seem justified several times over.

GOGOL'S FINAL PETERSBURG RESIDENCE
17 Malay Morskaya Ulitsa
🚇 *Nevsky Prospect/Gostiny Dvor*

Gogol lived in at least seven different apartments in St. Petersburg, most of which do not remain today. His last dwelling still stands, however, with a commemorative plaque documenting that Gogol lived here between 1833 and 1836 and wrote *The Government Inspector*, "The Nose," "Nevsky Prospect," and "Diary of a Madman" on the premises. The house is conveniently close to the Hermitage Museum and St. Isaac's Cathedral, among other marquee attractions. During the Soviet era the entire street bore Gogol's name, but it has since reverted to its prerevolutionary identity.

Sennaya Ploschad
(Haymarket Square)

A number of Gogol's residences were in the area around Sennaya Ploschad, or Haymarket Square. The neighborhood is now better known for its other resident writer, Fyodor Dostoevsky, who set most of his novel *Crime and Punishment* here. Gogol lived in the area in the late 1820s and early 1830s, well before Dostoevsky and before the industrial revolution that made the neighborhood a proletarian slum. But even in Gogol's day the neighborhood was noisy, crowded, and down-at-the-heels. Migrants from the provinces without much money, like Gogol himself, often found a place to live here. Tradesmen would work out of their apartments. Gogol noted that one of the buildings in which he lived also housed two tailors, a shoemaker, a maker of stockings, a man who repaired broken china, an interior decorator and painter, a confectioner, and a tobacco shop. "Naturally, the building is papered with golden advertising banners. I live on the fourth floor, but I feel that this is not a very good place for me."

In Gogol's story "The Portrait," the young artist Chartkov buys the cursed portrait of the moneylender at the Shchukin market on Sadovaya Ulitsa near Sennaya Ploschad, which was then one of the largest markets in St. Petersburg, with more than 250 stands selling everything from chickens to frying pans to boots. Today it's the site of Apraksin Dvor, a huge building from the 1860s full of stores selling clothes, shoes, and music. Behind the main building is an even bigger network of stalls and shacks and low-slung older buildings selling all kinds of dry goods. Unlike the shopping arcades on Nevsky Prospekt, Apraksin Dvor is downscale and untouristy. The vast expanse of stalls, the narrow, complicated alleyways, and the general din make this a site unlike any other in the city, and probably the closest one can get to imagining the place in Gogol's day.

Wintry Street on Vasilievsky Island, St. Petersburg, c. 1851

Vasilievsky Island

Gogol's Petersburg tales mention several outlying areas of the city. *The Portrait*'s Chartkov lives in an apartment on Vasilievsky Island. The island was then a working-class neighborhood, not seedy like Sennaya Ploschad but modest nonetheless. As soon as Chartkov comes into some money and sets himself up as a portrait painter for Petersburg high society, he moves to a much fancier apartment on Nevsky Prospekt—he can't very well invite society to pose in a studio on Vasilievsky Island.

Today Vasilievsky Island is a quiet residential area of older apartment buildings. On the Neva waterfront, at #7/9 Universitetskaya Naberezhnaya, stands St. Petersburg University. A friend of Gogol's helped him get a position as an adjunct professor of ancient and medieval history at the university in 1834, even though Gogol had no academic training or—it turned out—any particular talent as a lecturer. He lasted at the university less than two years; he was not much respected by the rest of the faculty, and in any case he grew bored with the lectures and quit the position to write full time.

ACADEMY OF ARTS MUSEUM
17 Universitetskaya Naberezhnaya
(812) 213-6496
🚇 *Vasileostrovskaya*
Wednesday–Sunday 11 am–7 pm;
closed Monday and Tuesday

Down the street from St. Petersburg University is the Academy of Arts, where, in the early 1830s, Gogol took painting classes in the evenings after work. He was no good, by his own description, but very much looked forward to the classes. Two of his Petersburg tales, "The Portrait" and "Nevsky Prospekt," have characters who are painters. In the latter he writes ironically of "an artist in the land of snows":

> These artists do not in the least resemble Italian artists—proud, ardent, like Italy and its sky; on the contrary they are for the most part kind and meek people...who drink tea with their two friends in a small room, who talk modestly about their favorite subject....

He is forever inviting some old beggar woman to his place and making her sit for a good six hours, so as to transfer her pathetic, insensible expression to canvas....They paint almost everything in dull, grayish colors, the indelible imprint of the north.

The Academy of Fine Arts is of course better known for its more talented graduates, and today it has a small museum exhibiting the work of current and former students of the last two hundred years, including the early work of the great late-nineteenth-century painter Ilya Repin.

Ivan Turgenev

IVAN
TURGENEV
1818–1883

*I*VAN TURGENEV WAS QUITE DIFFER-
ENT FROM THE TWO LITERARY GIANTS
who dominated Russian letters in the second half of
the nineteenth century, Tolstoy and Dostoevsky. Where-
as the other writers were opinionated, quarrelsome,
and self-important, Turgenev was mild-mannered and
self-effacing. Dostoevsky and Tolstoy often expressed
their views on politics and religion in their fiction, but
Turgenev's portraits of provincial gentry and student
radicals were so roundly sympathetic that his readers,
used to more didactic novels, had a hard time guess-
ing where his allegiances lay. In fact Turgenev, born to

a noble family in Oryol and educated in Moscow and Petersburg, was an ardent liberal who supported the abolition of serfdom and at times had sympathy for radical leftist revolutionaries. But he was not, by nature, an ideological writer. His characters came before his convictions, and novels like *A Sportsman's Sketches*, *Home of the Gentry*, and *Fathers and Sons* are masterpieces of careful observation of human relationships. His stories largely take place in the provinces, but Petersburg, where the writer lived for nearly thirty years, hovers just over the horizon: it's where his characters attend university, join the civil service, and meet their wives. Turgenev's depiction of the city can't be called fond—Petersburg is closely associated in his books with high-society sycophants who toady to the tsar and mindlessly imitate Western fashions. In *Home of the Gentry*, Ivan Lavretzky is sent to live in Petersburg with a rich old aunt who, "made up to the eyebrows and perfumed with scent à la Richelieu, surrounded by little Negro pages, short-legged dogs and shrieking parrots, died on a bent little Louis XV silk divan, with an enameled snuffbox by Petitot in her hand."

Turgenev often wrote about the clash of values between liberals of his generation and the more radical leftists who supplanted them. *Fathers and Sons* portrays a young, self-described "nihilist" who believes only in what can be proven rationally and is ready to give his life to help free the Caucasus region from Turkish occupation. The book was published in 1862. To Russian intellectuals of the time, literature was inextricable from social and political concerns, and novels were judged not only for their artistic qualities but also for the ideas they put forward about how to improve Russian society. *Fathers and Sons* was attacked from every part of the political spectrum. Some thought it was a vicious caricature of the radical left, others that it was an approving, overly romanticized portrait of it. Turgenev was so frustrated by the reception of the novel that in 1862 he left Russia for Europe. He spent the rest of his life in Baden-Baden and Paris, though he made regu-

Pauline Viardot-Garcia, 1859

lar visits to Petersburg and Moscow, continued to write about the Russian scene, and annoyed both the left and the right with every politically ambiguous novel he published. The fact that Turgenev abandoned his home country but presumed to keep writing about it was a sore point with his critics. He and Dostoevsky had a famous quarrel in which Dostoevsky told him he needed to get a telescope so that he could better see what was going on in Russia.

Turgenev's private life was no less intriguing. When he was twenty-five, Turgenev met and fell in love with the opera singer Pauline Viardot while she was visiting Petersburg (with her husband). They may or may not have had an affair, but certainly they struck up a friendship and she became his muse. Twenty years later, upon quitting Russia, Turgenev settled into the house next to the Viardots in Baden-Baden. It's not certain that he and Viardot were lovers, but there's no doubt that the attachment was intense on both sides. Viardot's husband seemed not to mind the relationship, whatever its nature. He was friendly with Turgenev and allowed him to stay on as their neighbor in Baden-Baden and Paris for the next twenty years.

SITES
Historic Center

SITE OF TURGENEV'S FORMER RESIDENCE
52 Ulitsa Mayakovskovo
 *Mayakovskaya*

While he was a student Turgenev lived with his older

brother on Shestilavochnaya Ulitsa, now called Ulitsa Mayakovskovo (in honor of the street's other resident writer, the poet Vladimir Mayakovsky (p. 101). By coincidence, the house where Turgenev lived stood roughly on the same plot of land where Mayakovsky's apartment was later built, at 52 Mayakovskaya Ulitsa. As a student Turgenev quickly became a presence at the city's literary gatherings. At a party given by one of his professors he met his idol, Alexander Pushkin. He later visited Pushkin on his deathbed after the duel, and when the poet died it was Turgenev who asked a servant to cut off a lock of the poet's hair, which is now on display at the Pushkin Memorial Flat (p. 22). Turgenev, in turn, later encouraged the work of younger writers like Leo Tolstoy, whom he hosted at his apartment at 38 Naberezhnaya reki Fontanki (p. 59) for three months after Tolstoy finished a tour of duty in Sebastopol.

Southern Suburbs

LITERATORSKIE MOSTKI, VOLKOV CEMETERY
30 Rasstannaya Ulitsa
(812) 166-2383
🚇 *Ligovsky Prospekt*
Daily 11 am–5 pm November–March, 11 am–7 pm April–October; closed Thursday

Shortly before he died of cancer in France in 1883, Turgenev asked to be buried in St. Petersburg near his great friend, the literary critic Vissarion Belinsky, in an elite section of the Volkov Cemetery called Literatorski Mostki (Literary Bridges). His tombstone is close not only to Belinsky's but also to the grave of the satirist Saltykov-Schedrin, Turgenev's critic and rival, and to Ivan Goncharov, another eminent nineteenth-century writer and author of the comic novel *Oblomov*, about an aristocrat too lazy to venture from his bed.

Fyodor Dostoevsky, 1872

FYODOR
DOSTOEVSKY
1821–1881

*F*YODOR DOSTOEVSKY'S CHARACTERS HAUNT ST. PETERSBURG. A FIRST-TIME visitor to the city can't help but think of Raskolnikov walking these streets muttering long soliloquies. Or she might think of the hapless clerk Golyadkin from *The Double*, who meets his exact replica walking home on a stormy night by the Fontanka River, or of the recluse in "White Nights" who falls in love for the first time during the long days of the summer solstice. In the second half of the nineteenth century Petersburg was a rapidly industrializing city swarming with new residents and new ideas for improving the human lot.

Dostoevsky's garrulous characters—"people whose lives are hanging out on their tongues," as the writer V. S. Pritchett put it—give voice to some of the impassioned intellectual debates of the time. This is particularly true of his great Petersburg antihero, *Crime and Punishment*'s Raskolnikov, who has spent too much time reading Western political philosophy and tries, disastrously, to apply bookish Western ideas to his own life. Dostoevsky was at first sympathetic, then furiously opposed to, the liberal utopian ideas from the West that became popular with mid-century intellectuals, and his great books—*Notes from Underground*, *Crime and Punishment*, *The Idiot*, *The Devils*, *The Brothers Karamazov*—are rebuttals to some of the most cherished progressive ideals of his fellow writers. But of course his books are much more than that: their characters have long outlived the nineteenth-century cultural ferment that spawned them, and today we're likely to feel that they give voice to some of the most pressing questions of our time.

Dostoevsky himself was a liberal idealist in his youth, and his devastating depictions of young men who read too much for their own good owes something to his own revolutionary past. His father was a doctor in a public hospital outside of Moscow, which made Dostoevsky one of the few Russian novelists of his era not to come from aristocracy. The elder Dostoevsky did make a fortune, however, and sent Fyodor to the military engineering school in Petersburg when he was sixteen. But the boy was more interested in novels than engineering. He finished school, did his compulsory two years of military service, and then turned entirely to writing.

The first book Dostoevsky wrote was *Poor Folk*, an epistolary novel in which a young seamstress forced to marry an unkind man for money corresponds with her friend, an equally poor civil servant who rents a small corner of a boardinghouse kitchen. "It's true that there are better—possibly much better—lodgings to be found," he writes, but this way he "can save enough to be able to afford both tea and sugar." The squalor Dostoevsky describes was not at all unusual at the time and was a source of concern among liberal reformers. Sentimental novels about the city's poor were much in vogue. Though *Poor Folk* seems flat today, especially compared to Dostoevsky's later work, it showed far more artistry and sympathy for its plebian characters than other such social novels. When the book came out in 1846, Dostoevsky was welcomed into the company (and the comfortable houses) of the country's most respected writers: Ivan Turgenev, Ivan Goncharov, Mikhail Saltykov-Schedrin. But, like some of his most memorable characters, Dostoevsky was painfully self-conscious and struck others as irritable and unpleasantly sarcastic. He alienated the people who were trying to help him in his career, and he soon stopped receiving invitations.

Devastated by his social failures and the chilly response to his second novel, *The Double*, Dostoevsky found company in a more actively political society. The Petrashevsky circle was a loose association of hundreds of students, writers, landowners, merchants, and other Petersburgers of varied backgrounds who met weekly to argue about political philosophy and ideas for social reform. On the whole it was more a discussion group than a political organization, but Dostoevsky became involved in a small, radical subgroup that was plotting violent revolution. When the Petrashevksy circle was infiltrated by the tsar's secret police, Dostoevsky and his were comrades particularly vulnerable.

On April 23, 1849, Dostoevsky was awakened at three in the morning by the secret police, who took him to their headquarters on the Fontanka River. Other members were being corralled there from all over the city. They were eventually taken to cells in the Peter and Paul fortress, where they were interrogated and tried over a period of months. Fifteen members of the circle were sentenced to death. Dostoevsky was one of them. On execution day, December 22, the condemned men were led to a public square, Semyonovsky Platz, where the firing squad was supposed to do its work. Just as the first three convicts were to be shot, an official announced that the tsar had commuted their sentences to hard labor in Siberia.

Dostoevsky's life was effectively split in two by his arrest and exile. The experience of the mock execution was unnerving, to say the least (one of the other condemned men died of a heart attack on the spot, and another went insane). Afterward, Dostoevsky spent six years in prison camps in the Siberian city of Omsk, then had four years of forced army service. In the prison camps he lived not only with political prisoners but with ordinary criminals, many of whom had committed murder. He had imagined that in the barracks, where upper- and lower-class prisoners shared the same official status, a sort of brotherhood might emerge. Instead, the peasant criminals loathed the "gentlemen" and were generally amoral, stealing from the gentle-

The Hay Square, c. 1840

men and from each other freely, fighting brutally, and showing no remorse for their crimes. Yet they had unexpected moments of piety that impressed Dostoevsky. Even callous criminals seemed reverent and respectful of one another at the prison camp's Easter service. This spark of spirituality (or so Dostoevsky interpreted it) became the basis of a new philosophy of his, which held that the only way to improve the lives of the lower classes (and the upper, too), was to cultivate religious feeling. Rational social reform could never stamp out man's destructive urges, he decided. Only the example of Jesus Christ and faith in God could inspire people to conquer their worst impulses.

He returned to St. Petersburg from Siberia ready to pour these new ideas into his writing. He had lost much of his nervousness, hypochondria, and shyness during the ordeals of the previous decade, and he set to work with a new confidence and sense of urgency.

There was another reason that Dostoevsky's last fifteen years were the most productive time of his life: his improbably efficient new wife. In the mid-1860s, a few years after his return from Siberia, Dostoevsky was working all hours of the day to finish *Crime and Punishment*. But he needed more money, so he signed a reckless contract with his publisher: he had to produce a wholly new novel from scratch in four weeks. If he failed to deliver, all his earnings for the next nine years would revert to the publisher.

He needed someone who could type. The stenographer's office sent him Anna Snitkina, one of few women in a still mostly male profession. The choice was fortuitous: Snitkina, it turned out, had read and loved Dostoevsky's work—and this was years before he became famous among ordinary Petersburgers. With Snitkina's help he was able to finish dictating the new novel, *The Gambler*, in time to avoid the penalty, and also completed *Crime and Punishment* later that month. They soon married and eventually had four children, two of whom died young. Anna would be his lifelong secretary, accountant, and housekeeper.

Crime and Punishment was a huge success. The plot was based on an actual murder that had taken place in Petersburg, one that many of his readers would have remembered from the papers. (Dostoevsky regularly pored over newspapers looking for interesting crimes, and the murders in *The Brothers Karamazov* and *Devils* are also inspired by real-life killings.) Superficially disguised as a detective story, the novel was a psychologically complex and ambiguous portrait of a murderer wholly new in fiction. Dostoevsky had been interested in writing an account of a murder since his prison term, and he wove into the novel the criticisms of liberal, individualist ideology that he had begun to formulate in Siberia. But it is Petersburg itself that gives shape to Raskolnikov's story, throwing unexpected detours in his way and leading him to chance encounters with strangers in its streets and taverns. Sometimes the city itself seems to be urging Raskolnikov on to murder: "Lime, scaffolding, bricks, dust everywhere, and that special summer stench known so well to every Petersburger who cannot afford to rent a summer house—all at once these things unpleasantly shook the young man's already overwrought nerves." The chaos and evil that thrive in Dostoevsky's Petersburg make a mockery of Peter's noble ideal of a rationally planned city.

Much of the book takes place in Raskolnikov's humble neighborhood near the haymarket, which is the setting for some of the book's most wrenching scenes of poverty and degradation, but also for redemption: Raskolnikov kneels in the middle of the haymarket to beg God forgiveness for his crime. Petersburg's majestic avenues and mansions, on the other hand, have little to do with the real life of the city in this novel. For Raskolnikov they are simply alienating and even have a sinister air. "An inexplicable chill" overcomes him while he's standing on the Nikolaevsky Bridge (now called Most Leytanenta Schmidta) looking out at the beautiful panorama of the Winter Palace, waterfront mansions, and the dome of St. Isaac's Cathedral. "It seemed to him that at that moment he had cut himself off, as with scissors, from everyone and everything."

A different Petersburg is the setting for *The Idiot*, which follows the saintly Prince Myshkin as he reenters Russian society after spending much of his boyhood and youth in a Swiss sanatorium. Petersburg society is corrupting: the prince quickly falls in love with two different women. Over one of them, he and his friend Rogozhin become violent rivals. Most of the characters in *The Idiot* are aristocratic or rich or both.

General Yepanchin, the prince's benefactor, owns a house "just off Liteiny [Prospect], towards the Church of the Transfiguration," a prosperous part of the city. He also has a country estate in Pavlovsk, a town near Petersburg that was a retreat for the royals and the rich. The first railway in Russia, built in 1837, connected Petersburg and Pavlovsk, making the latter a popular day trip for anyone who could afford the tickets. The princes and generals in *The Idiot* regularly decamp to summer houses in Pavlovsk—Prince Myshkin's milieu can afford to leave Petersburg at will. Compared to *Crime and Punishment*, the city in *The Idiot* is far less claustrophobic for its characters and, perhaps as a result, somewhat less vivid for its readers. This may be because Dostoevsky wrote *The Idiot* while traveling in Switzerland and Italy in the late 1860s, where he and his wife had gone to escape their Petersburg debts.

Dostoevsky's two other great novels, *Devils* and *The Brothers Karamazov*, have little to do with Petersburg, but they circle around the same problems and questions that Dostoevsky raised in *Crime and Punishment*: the presence of evil in the world, the inadequacy of liberal reforms in confronting it, and the best ways to help the most troubled and the most vulnerable members of society. His books continued to be much read and discussed for the rest of Dostoevsky's life. When he had a heart attack in January 1881, Petersburgers gathered at his apartment to hold a vigil. He died a few days later.

SITES

In the twenty-eight years that he lived in St. Petersburg, Dostoevsky moved twenty times and never spent more than three years in any one apartment. He preferred to live in buildings situated on corners—he liked intersections and multiple perspectives—and had two favorite neighborhoods where many of his former dwellings are concentrated: one is the area around Sennaya Ploschad (Haymarket Square), and the other is Vladmirskaya. They were both shabby neighborhoods, and Dostoevsky lived in them partly out of sheer financial necessity. But he was also fascinated by the street life in the rough parts of St. Petersburg, and he trailed people on the sidewalks and took careful notes on what he saw.

Sennaya Ploschad

Sennaya Ploschad, or Haymarket Square, was the site of the city's haymarket in Dostoevsky's time, where peasants would come to sell hay and produce from the countryside. The square and the neighborhood around it were a crossroads for all manner of Petersburg's downtrodden. Taverns and brothels lined the streets around the square. Low-rent apartment buildings housed students, artisans, peddlers, small-time shop-keepers, clerks, servants, and prostitutes. A scene from *Crime and Punishment* describes an alley near Sennaya Ploschad full of shabbily dressed prostitutes calling out blandishments to men passing by in the street. "Some were over forty, but there were some younger than seventeen; almost every one of them had a black eye."

Today Sennaya Ploshad is still crowded and clamorous, but the commercial activity is somewhat more reputable, with a sleek mall and stands selling DVDs and fast food. The neighborhood around the square is dominated by stores and outdoor markets, including the giant Apraksin Dvor. The residential streets are narrow and treeless. In Soviet times the neighborhood contained some of the most crowded and poorly equipped communal apartments. There are still a small number of communal apartments left, some of which local government uses to house rehabilitated alcoholics and drug users from halfway houses.

DOSTOEVSKY'S FORMER RESIDENCES
Kaznacheyskaya Ulitsa, Nos. 1, 7, and 9
🚇 *Sennaya Ploschad/Sadovaya*

Dostoevsky lived in three different residences on Kaznacheyskaya Ulitsa in the 1860s: Nos. 1, 7, and 9. The street was then called Malaya Meschanskaya, or Petit Bourgeois street, a testament to the commercial activity that took place there. At No. 7, where Dostoevsky lived between August 1864 and January 1867, he finished *Crime and Punishment* and wrote *The Gambler* with the help of his stenographer (and soon-to-be second wife) Anna Snitkina.

Crime and Punishment is largely set in this neighborhood. Though Dostoevsky didn't spell out the full names of the streets, he described the streets and buildings very precisely. It's almost certain that Raskolnikov's garret apartment ("more like a cupboard than a room") was in the building at No. 5 or No. 9 Stolyarniy Pereulok. The saintly prostitute Sonya Marmeladov lived at either No. 63 or No. 73 on the Griboedov Canal Embankment. Raskolnikov's victim, the old lady pawnbroker, lived farther down Griboedov Canal Embankment at No. 104.

Scenes in *The Idiot* are also set near Sennaya Ploschad. Rogozhin, the rich merchant's son who befriends and then menaces Prince Myshkin, lives "on Gorokhovaya Street, not far from Sadovaya," in a "large, gloomy, three-storied house, devoid of architectural pretension, and of a dirty-green colour." It's in Rogozhin's house that Myshkin makes a pact with Rogozhin not to visit Nastasya Filipovna—a pact he eventually breaks, leading to her murder and to his own descent into dementia.

Vladimirskaya

Vladimirskaya is a neighborhood named after the recently restored Vladimir Church. Across the street, at the intersection of Vladimirsky Prospect, Kuznechniy Pereulok, and Bolshaya Mosckovskaya Ulitsa, stands a statue of Dostoevsky. Vladimirsky Prospect, the neighborhood's main artery, is full of new stores and eateries, but the quiet sidestreets are mostly untouched by renovation and have some spectacularly decrepit-looking apartment buildings.

DOSTOEVSKY'S FORMER RESIDENCE
11 Vladmirsky Prospect
🚇 *Vladimirskaya/Dostoevskaya*

These were Dostoevsky's first lodgings after he left the military academy. He rented a single room in an apartment on the second floor, furnished only with an old sofa, some chairs, and a desk at which he wrote his first novel, *Poor Folk*.

DOSTOEVSKY MEMORIAL MUSEUM
5/2 Kuznechny Pereulok
(812) 311-4031
🚇 *Vladimirskaya/Dostoevskaya*
Daily 11 am–6 pm; closed Monday and
the last Wednesday of each month

The museum is in Dostoevsky's last apartment, where he lived with Anna and their two children from October 1878 until his death two and a half years later. The couple's third child, Alexei, had died of an epileptic seizure in the spring of 1878, and they moved into this apartment largely to escape the difficult memories associated with their previous home. The building is the original one in which the Dostoevskys lived, but the apartment had not been preserved. It was later restored based on photos, drawings, and the many documents that Anna painstakingly saved after Dostoevsky's death. A few original items do remain: Dostoevsky's hat, for instance, and a tobacco box on which his daughter had written "January 28, 1881—Papa died."

SEMYONOVSKIY PLATS
Zagorodny Prospect, between
Zvenigorodskaya Ulitsa and Podyezdnoi Pereulok
🚇 *Tekhnologichesky Institut*

Now a quiet park called Pionerskaya Ploschad, this square was the site of Dostoevsky's mock execution. He and other members of the Petrashevsky circle were sentenced to death for treason and brought here to be shot before the assembled crowd. The first three prisoners were tied to a stake and blindfolded. Just before the firing squad fired their shots a messenger announced that Tsar Nicholas I had commuted their sentence to hard labor—the fake execution proceedings had been an elaborate form of torture dreamed up by the tsar to punish the prisoners. Dostoevsky spent four years doing hard labor at a work camp in the Siberian city of Omsk, and several more years in compulsory military service.

TRINITY CATHEDRAL
Troistky Prospect at the corner of
Izmailovsky Prospect
🚇 *Tekhnologichesky Institut*

Not to be confused with the Trinity Cathedral inside the Alexander Nevsky Monastery, this church with spectacular blue domes is where Dostoevsky married Anna Snitkina. Like many Orthodox Churches, it was shut down under Stalin's reign and did not open again until perestroika.

Historic Center

MIKHAILOVSKY CASTLE
(Engineers' Castle)
2 Sadovaya Ulitsa
(812) 210-4173
🚇 *Nevsky Prospect/Gostiny Dvor*
Daily 10 am–6 pm; closed Tuesdays

This palace was built at the end of the eighteenth century by Tsar Paul I, who was so afraid of assassination plots that he dug a moat around the palace to hold back intruders. He felt so safe in this castle, however, that he dismissed most of his armed guards. In March 1801, only forty days after he moved into the supposedly impregnable new home, a group of government conspirators broke into the castle and strangled him. The castle later became an engineering school. Dostoevsky enrolled at the age of sixteen and lived between 1838 and 1841 in the building dormitory, where students liked to tell stories of Paul's ghost haunting the castle. Today the castle is part of the Russian Museum and contains a portrait gallery and temporary exhibition rooms.

DOSTOEVSKY'S FORMER RESIDENCE
8 Voznesensky Prospect
(at the corner of Malaya Morskaya)
🚇 *Nevsky Prospect/Gostiny Dvor*

Dostoevsky was sleeping in his apartment here on April 23, 1849, when he was awakened by a dreaded knock at the door: the police had come to arrest him for participating in the dissident social group called the Petrashevsky circle. The writer had lived at this address for two years before his arrest, during which time he wrote "White Nights," his most romantic and bittersweet Petersburg story.

Petrograd Side

PETER AND PAUL FORTRESS
(812) 238-0511
🚇 *Gorkovskaya*
Hours: Monday and Thursday–Sunday 10 am–6 pm;
Tuesday 10 am–5 pm; closed Wednesday; grounds
remain open daily until midnight

The fortress was the first building erected in the city. Peter the Great converted part of the complex into a political prison soon after it was built, and its brutal conditions were infamous by the time Dostoevsky was brought here in 1849. For eight months he lived in a cell in the Secret House, a special high-security area within a building called the Alexeevsky Ravelin (also called the Alexis Ravelin), reserved for political prisoners that the tsar considered most threatening.

The Soviets turned the fortress complex into a museum, and several different exhibits, as well as the Peter and Paul Cathedral, are contained within its walls. The original Alexeevsky Ravelin was demolished in 1884, and a building containing administrative offices now stands in its place, still identified on maps as the Alexeevsky Ravelin. Visitors who want a taste of prison life, however, can tour the Trubetskoy Bastion, another tsarist-era jail.

THE DAY BEFORE

*T*HOUGH MUCH OF *CRIME AND PUNISH-MENT* TAKES PLACE IN THE NEIGHBOR-hood near Sennaya Ploschad, Raskolnikov's feverish wanderings take him farther afield. The morning before he commits his murder, for instance, he crosses roughly half the city on foot, lost in a "whirlwind of thoughts" as he contemplates the murder he has been planning for a month. His long route can still be traced on foot today (though only hardy pedestrians with a lot of time in the city will want to do the whole thing) and leads from the clamorous commercial neighborhood around Sennaya Ploschad past some of the most beautiful streets of the city center, through quiet residential neighborhoods and lush public parks. Raskolnikov leaves his apartment on Stolyarniy Pereulok and walks up Voznesensky Prospect, talking to himself so excitedly that he is mistaken for a drunk. On Konnogvardeisky Boulevard he tries to protect a drunken teenage streetwalker from a lecher, then makes his way to Vasilievsky Island, where he once attended Petersburg University before running out of tuition money, and where his university friend Razumikhin still lives. He means to visit Razumikhin but he's so distracted by racing thoughts that he walks all the way across the tip of Vasilievsky Island, crosses over to the Petrograd side of the city, and heads toward what Petersburgers refer to as "the islands," meaning the three small, verdant islands north of the Petrograd side, called Krestovsky, Yelagin, and Kamenny Islands. Nineteenth-century swells had their dachas, or summer houses, on these islands, and to this day they remain the greenest parts of St. Petersburg, now mostly public park land. Here Raskolnikov finds an eating-house and has a glass of vodka and a "pie with some sort of filling." He starts for home but the vodka "affected him at once," and he has to take a nap under a bush on Petrovsky Island, part of the Petrograd side of the city (now home to sports stadiums and parks), where he has a terrifying dream that resembles a crucial episode from Dostoevsky's own childhood: he is a small boy walking through his provincial village when he sees a group of men beating a horse to death out of pure bloodlust. The shaken Raskolnikov wakes up and heads for home by way of the Tuchkov Bridge, resolving that he will not commit murder. But just before he gets home, an unexpected detour through Sennaya Ploschad changes his fate: he overhears that the moneylender's sister is supposed to be out of the house the following evening—the perfect opportunity to get the moneylender alone and kill her, he thinks, is too good to pass up.

Svidrigailov, the murderer and libertine who is Raskolnikov's shadowy double, traces a similar journey at the end of the novel as he prepares to commit suicide: he goes to Vasilievsky Island (to say goodbye to his fiancée, who lives at the corner of 3-ya Linia and Maly Prospect), crosses the Tuchkov Bridge (pausing to look down into the water "with some special curiosity") to the Petrograd side, gets food, drink, and a room for the night in a hotel, then wakes from a nightmare and resolves to kill himself on Petrovsky Island. But on his way there he changes his mind and does the deed on a nondescript patch of sidewalk in front of a watchtower, so that there will be at least one "official witness."

◆

THE MURDER

The day of the actual murder Raskolnikov stays closer to home, in the Sennaya Ploschad neighborhood. Having rehearsed the murder route several times over the last month, he knows that it's exactly 730 steps from the gate of his building on Stolyarniy Pereulok ("S-----y Lane" in English translations of the book) to the moneylender's apartment. He leaves his building and walks down Stolyarniy Pereulok to the Griboedov Canal (known then as the Ekaterinsky Canal). He crosses the canal by the Kokushkin Bridge and turns right onto Sadovaya Ulitsa. He walks by the Yusupov Garden, an estate of the Yusupov family, one of the most prominent and richest of the nineteenth century (today the mansion and its grounds are a public park), then quickly bears right on Prospect Rimskogo-Korsakova. A few blocks later he has arrived at the moneylender's building, 104 Griboedov Canal Embankment. Today the apartment houses along the canal are lovely (if badly in need of fresh paint), but a peek into some of the dilapidated inner courtyards will evoke Dostoevskian squalor. Raskolnikov walks through the gate at No. 104 into the inner courtyard (a big, noisy hay wagon fortuitously drives through the gate at the same instant and gives Raskolnikov cover from passersby). The moneylender lives on the fourth floor, at apartment No. 74, a small room "with yellow paper, geraniums, and muslin curtains" whose windows are closed "despite the stuffiness." Two murders later, Raskolnikov exits the building through the back tunnel leading to Srednaya Podyacheskaya Ulitsa.

✦

THE NEXT DAY

Half delirious with guilt and terror, Raskolnikov resolves to dump the loot that he took from the moneylender into the Ekaterinsky (now Griboedov) Canal. But it was a busy waterway in those days, and when he gets there he realizes there would be too many witnesses: "rafts were standing there and washer-women were doing laundry on them," boats were moored along the edges and "people were simply swarming all over the place." Instead, he walks up Voznesensky Prospect and, on a whim, ends up putting the loot under a stone in the courtyard of a building on Isaakievskaya Ploschad.

Leo Tolstoy

LEO TOLSTOY
1828-1910

*L*EO TOLSTOY DID NOT SPEND MUCH
TIME IN PETERSBURG, BUT HE HAD
very strong opinions about the city: it stood for everything he hated about Russian aristocratic life. In his
novels the capital is a city of posers and sycophants. He
was a keen observer of the differences in manners, cus-
toms, and fashions between Petersburg and Moscow,
and Peter's city inevitably comes out the loser in his
comparisons of the two great capitals, for only one of
them, in his view, is authentically Russian.

The writer was born and raised on his family's
country estate, Yasnaya Polyana, about 120 miles south
of Moscow. He moved to Petersburg as a young man in
1849 to take his law exams, but he left the capital the

following year, having run up such a huge gambling debt that he had to sell part of the family estate to cover it. He spent three more months in Petersburg in 1855.

Tolstoy was not happy in the capital. He disapproved of the decadent habits of Petersburg's aristocracy, and of his own susceptibility to them—his weaknesses for gambling, sex, and drinking were deeply vexing to him. It was in 1855, around the time of his stay in Petersburg, that he began formulating his ideas about a new kind of spirituality, a Christianity "purged of dogmatism and mysticism; a practical religion not promising future bliss, but giving bliss on earth." Petersburg society, he felt, was particularly lacking in spiritual values and placed only immoral temptations in the way of its members. In *War and Peace*, young Petersburg men who spend too much money or get involved in dissolute hijinks are sent by their families to sleepy Moscow, where they can't get into so much trouble.

Geography is destiny in *War and Peace*: the city in which characters grow up can determine their facial expressions and vocabulary, their spontaneity and their capacity for emotion and sympathy. Anna Scherer, the doyenne of Petersburg high society, uses the latest fashionable French words and has no real emotions, only feigned enthusiasms. She runs her salon mechanically, like the "foreman of a spinning mill." Her eminent guest, Prince Vasily Kuragin, is "a wound-up clock, saying by force of habit things he did not even expect to be believed." The Rostov family of Moscow practices a different kind of hospitality: huge, merry dinners for as many as eighty people, no formal invitations required. Their delightfully spontaneous and charming teenage daughter, Countess Natasha Rostova, gets noticed when she visits Petersburg because "there's something fresh, original, un-Petersburg-like about her."

In *Anna Karenina*, Tolstoy is even more explicit in summing up the differences between Petersburg and Moscow. Through the thoughts of Stepan Oblonsky, he conveys, with irony, the trouble with Petersburg:

When [Stepan Arkadyich Oblonsky] lived in Moscow for a long time without leaving, he reached the point of worrying about his wife's bad moods and reproaches, his children's health and education, the petty concerns of his [civil] service; he even worried about having debts. But he needed only to go and stay for a while in Petersburg, in the circle to which he belonged…and immediately all these thoughts vanished and melted away like wax before the face of fire.

Wife?…Only that day he had been talking with Prince Chechensky. Prince Chechenksy had a wife and family…and there was another illegitimate family, in which there were also children. Though the first family was good as well, Prince Chechensky felt happier in the second family.…What would they have said to that in Moscow?

He may be a bit rough on the Petersburgers, but Tolstoy's observations are rooted in cultural differences that had solidified between Petersburg and Moscow in the nineteenth century. Court life, with its inherent formality and sycophancy, dominated Petersburg society, while Moscow social life could remain more spontaneous away from the eye of the tsar. And with its history of isolationism, Moscow had not gone as far as Petersburg in adopting the styles of the West. To Petersburgers, Moscow seemed provincial. But to Tolstoy and other Moscow partisans, a Russian could never feel at home in Petersburg.

TOLSTOY'S TEMPORARY RESIDENCE
38 Naberzhnaya reki Fontanki (near Nevsky Prospect)
 *Mayakovskaya*

Tolstoy came through the capital after he had finished a tour fighting the Turks in Sebastopol. He had already published *Childhood* and *Boyhood*, two of his auto-biographical books. His work caught the eye of Ivan Turgenev, who invited Tolstoy to stay with him for several months at his apartment on the Fontanka River and introduced him to all his literary friends in the city. ("Turgenev is a bore," Tolstoy wrote in his diary.) Today a plaque on the building, which also houses the English-language bookstore Angliya, commemorates Tolstoy's visit.

Alexander Blok, 1907

ALEXANDER BLOK
1880–1921

OR MANY RUSSIANS, ALEXANDER BLOK IS THE COUNTRY'S SECOND MOST IM-portant poet after Pushkin. Unfortunately for English readers, Blok's poems, written in rhymed and metered verse, have a musical quality that's hopelessly difficult to reproduce in translation. They also express a romantic sensibility that can seem overwrought when rendered in English.

Blok was the most talented member of a generation of Russian poets called Symbolists, who were fascinated with mystical experiences and irrational impulses (Dostoevsky was their muse). Many of Blok's early poems are intimations of other worlds ("The pine trees imprison me in their dark destiny,/but unmistakably there comes the sound/of a far distant, undiscovered city") or describe an idealized female figure representing divine wisdom, whom he called the Beautiful Lady (it sounds grander in Russian). His Petersburg is one of wild Gogolian storms, frozen rivers and "sapphire acres under snow."

Having neglected poetry for decades in favor of the well-meaning social novel, Russian readers and writers joyfully rediscovered verse at the end of the nineteenth century. Russia had its own decadent *fin de siècle*, which, like the Western version, celebrated art for art's sake, as well as free love, opium, cabarets, and the pageantry of city life. But being Russian, the Symbolist poets were still preoccupied by the fate of the their country, which they tended to see in apocalyptic terms. A popular idea among the Symbolists, which Blok shared, was that Russia would soon be purged of corruption and spiritually redeemed by a dreadful, looming disaster.

Blok was born in 1880 in the rector's house of St. Petersburg University, where his maternal grandfather, a respected botanist, was rector and his father was a law professor. They were a privileged and cultured family, and Blok started writing poetry as a boy.

The Bloks divorced when Alexander was young. His mother married an army officer and, when Blok was nine, mother and son moved into the military barracks on the Petrograd side of the city where her new husband lived. To young Blok it felt like the provinces. The streets, many of them still unpaved in 1889 when the family moved, were lined with small wooden houses with little gardens out front.

But as Blok was growing up, the neighborhood began to fill with factories and apartment buildings to house the new industrial workers. Blok's windows looked out onto one of the new factories, and he wrote a poem about workers gathering for the evening shift at the gates, waiting to be let in while, from a perch on the wall, "someone motionless, someone black/is silently counting them all." The turn of the century was a boom time for Petersburg, and the humbleness of Blok's neighborhood couldn't have been more different from the prosperity of the city center, where fancy shops full of delicacies were opening to serve newly rich industrialists. Of course, the new bourgeoisie didn't buy only Parisian dresses and imported snuff boxes, but also books, paintings, and tickets to plays and concerts. Their patronage led to a period of great artistic ferment among writers and artists who, for their part, looked down on their bourgeois patrons as philistines. Blok always said that he hated Nevsky Prospect and its self-satisfied swells. He was drawn instead to the factories, sprawling parks, and "dusty side-streets" of the city's edges. One of his most famous poems, "The Stranger," is set in a seedy bar in one of these outlying neighborhoods, where "the air is hot and strangely cloying,/and shouts drift from the drunkards' haunts/on the putrid breath of spring." The drunk narrator of the poem is entranced by a whore who comes in at the same time each evening, whose "nodding ostrich-feather plume/begins to hypnotize my brain."

In his early twenties, Blok married Liubov Mendeleyeva, a much-admired Petersburg beauty (and the daughter of Russia's great chemist, Dmitri Mendeleyev, who developed the periodic table of elements). Blok's friend Andrei Bely (p. 71) later fell in love with Liubov himself, and he pursued her affections with a frank intensity that led to the end of the men's friendship. But Blok's own attraction to Liubov was said to be largely platonic. He admired her as an incarnation of the Beautiful Lady, and she was the muse and inspiration for many of his early poems, but their attachment seems not to have been a passionate one.

Blok's first poems appeared in literary magazines when he was in his early twenties, and he quickly became well known in Petersburg through his readings at private literary salons in the city. He was a charismatic and striking man, with huge pale eyes, dark skin, and a wide, romantic mouth. His picture appeared on postcards. Readers scrutinized his poems for clues to his personal life and formed "Blok societies" in which his poetry was read aloud and discussed. Young women were particularly captivated by the poet and would sometimes secretly follow him as he walked around the city. The teenage Anna Akhmatova (p. 79) was among his swooning fans. When she began to publish her own poetry she and Blok were constantly rumored to be having an affair—a rumor that they encouraged by dedicating poems to one another. Blok's poem "To Anna Akhmatova" begins,

> I sent you a rose in a glass of champagne
> while the gypsies played as the gypsies do.
> Then you turned to the man you were
> with and said:
> "You see his eyes? He's in love with me too."

A few years after his first poems were published, Blok became disillusioned with Petersburg intellectual life. The rituals and pretensions of the Symbolists came to seem unforgivably self-involved and isolated from the way that most Russians lived. He was sympathetic to the failed 1905 revolution, and his poetry became more melancholy and starkly realistic with passing years. "Night, street, a lamp, a chemist's window,/a senseless and dim light. No doubt/in a quarter century or so/there'll be no change. There's no way out."

Blok found little to admire in city life. Petersburg, as he saw it, was a place where men were constantly tempted to follow their worst impulses. He certainly did—readers who followed his personal life had no shortage of love affairs and drinking binges to gossip about. "I am nailed to a bar with liquor," begins one poem. "Been drunk all day. So what! I've lost/my happiness—gone in a troika/careering into silver mist."

He welcomed the overthrow of the tsar and the establishment of the liberal Provisional Government in February 1917. He even supported the Bolshevik coup that took place eight months later—not because he particularly believed in their principles but because he thought the Communist revolution would somehow lead Russia to spiritual renewal. He wrote an ode to the revolution called "The Twelve," about a group of Red Guards marching through the city in a blizzard. Fires burn all around them and the sounds of gunfire punctuate their conversations. They are coarse and carelessly brutal—one accidentally shoots a prostitute while aiming for the fellow who's walking with her. They spur each other on with revolutionary slogans. At the end of the poem Blok reveals that marching ahead of them, "carrying a blood-red flag," is Jesus Christ.

"The Twelve" was the first serious literary work about the revolution. Everyone read it and had some criticism to make: the Bolsheviks and their supporters disapproved of its Christian imagery, while most of Blok's friends in the intelligentsia thought that Blok's romantic ideas about the revolution were muddleheaded. But few disputed the poem's brilliance. Its thrilling staccato rhythms, its brutal images, and its use of street slang and new Communist jargon were wholly original and stirring—even for those who didn't particularly want to be stirred.

The revolution left Petersburg in chaos. The tsar, his family, and his court were gone, and so were the hundreds of uniformed officers, guards, and civil servants whose presence had so dominated Petersburg for two hundred years. The rich and middle class were no longer visible on the streets, and the fancy shops that served them shut down. For ordinary workers—the majority of the Petersburg's population—there was a vertiginous sense of freedom, and foreboding as well—no one believed that the new regime would last.

Lenin, who had led the Bolsheviks in their coup, moved the country's capital to Moscow in 1918. Nearly the whole state bureaucracy vanished from Petersburg. The city's economy shrank catastrophically, and many workers lost their jobs. Only people who worked at factories or in the few remaining government offices actually made any money. Everyone else received daily bread rations from the government. And because provisions were slow to come from the countryside, most of Petersburg went hungry.

Despite the deprivation, cultural events continued around Petersburg—plays, readings, and exhibitions, all dominated by avant-garde artists and sometimes staged in the streets and squares. Literary readings became even more important as the only means by which writers could share their new work, as book publishing had stopped during the civil war that followed the Bolshevik coup. The city itself had become stage and canvas, and for a few years it felt as though the cultural utopia that writers and artists had been dreaming of might really come to pass. The new government, for its part, reached out to writers and artists in these early years after the revolution. Blok was given a job with Ministry of Culture. He lectured on poetry and served on the editorial board of Vsemirnaya Literatura (World Literature) Publishing House, which compiled a list of all the great works that had to be translated into Russian for the education of the proletariat.

But this benevolence was short-lived. As the Bolsheviks strengthened their hold on the country they no longer needed the help of writers and artists, whom they began to view as threats to their authority. A philistine Soviet bureaucracy, concerned with ideological purity rather than artistic quality, took control of the funding of the arts. Worse, writers who were not avowedly Marxist came under the scrutiny of the secret police. Blok was arrested in February 1919 and interrogated about counterrevolutionary activities. He was not charged and was released the next day.

He stopped writing poetry and became gravely ill—not with one particular disease, but a physical malaise that seemed somehow an expression of his disappointment with the revolution and the end of Petersburg cultural life as he had known it. His former support of the revolution made the aftermath all the harder for him to accept. The revolutionary Leon Trotsky wrote of him, "Blok is not one of us, but he came towards us. And that is what broke him." Lenin wouldn't give him permission to go abroad for treatment, relenting only when it was clearly too late to save Blok's life.

In the summer of 1921, while Blok was dying, the Cheka made a wave of arrests in Petersburg, taking in hundreds of people and focusing on the intelligentsia: writers, academics, artists, and scientists. The pretext was a flimsy rumor about their participation in an armed resistance movement; the goal was to intimidate them into staying quiet about the failures of the Bolshevik regime, which were becoming increasingly clear as the city continued to starve.

SITES
Kolomna
—————————————

BLOK MUSEUM
57 Ulitsa Dekabristov
(812) 113-8616
🚇 *Sadovaya/Sennaya Ploschad*
Thursday–Monday 11 am–5 pm, Tuesday until 4 pm;
closed Wednesday and the last Tuesday of each month

Blok lived at this address the last nine years of his life, from 1912 to 1921, mostly in apartment 21, an elegant five-room residence with a view of the Pryazhka Canal that has been preserved as he and his wife, Liubov, left it. Blok was said to have kept his study, where he wrote "The Twelve," remarkably tidy. Papers were never strewn around, recalled the literary critic Kornei Chukovsky, a frequent guest at this apartment, and domestic items seemed to "arrange themselves at right angles around Blok." Visitors will see one of his favorite possessions on his desk: a ceramic ashtray in the form of a little white dachshund with red eyes. The last few years of his life Blok was involved in an exhausting battle with Soviet housing authorities to keep their apartment from being carved up into communal housing. He and Liubov lost the fight and had to move

in with Blok's mother and stepfather, who lived in No.
23, a smaller apartment in the same building, also part
of the museum.

Historic Center

GIPPIUS'S SALON
24 Liteiny Prospect
🚇 *Chernyshevskaya*

The most prestigious literary salon of Blok's day was
held at the apartment of the poet Zinaida Gippius
and her husband, the critic and scholar Dmitri Merezhkovsky. The couple dominated literary social life at
the turn of the century, and Gippius in particular—
tall, languorous, dressed in men's clothing or scan-
dalously tight dresses—was seen as one of the most
important arbiters of modernist writing. An invita-
tion to her salon, held Sundays after midnight, could
secure a writer's reputation. Blok appeared here for the
first time in 1902 to hear a lecture by Merezhkovsky,
and over the next few years became a regular visitor,
though he later came to despise the affectations of the
hosts and writers.

Smolny

VYACHESLAV IVANOV'S
FORMER RESIDENCE ("The Tower")
35 Tavricheskaya Ulitsa
(at the corner of Tverskaya Ulitsa)
🚇 *Chernyshevskaya*

Another prominent Symbolist salon was led by the
literature scholar Vyacheslav Ivanov. It was held on
Wednesdays from midnight to dawn in his seventh-
floor apartment, which looked out over the Tauride
Gardens and was affectionately known as the Tower.
The meetings would begin with lectures on philosophical subjects ("collective individualism," for example, or

"Christ and Antichrist") and end with poetry readings. The great literary critic Kornei Chukovsky recalls in his memoirs a particular night at the Tower that took place during white nights and culminated with the participants climbing out onto the roof to listen to Blok read "The Stranger": "Intoxicated by poetry and wine—and in those days poetry was as intoxicating as wine—we emerged under the white sky, and Blok, slowly, with outward calm, and young and tanned (he was always tanned by early spring), climbed onto the large iron frame used for telephone lines, and as if leading us in prayer recited three or four times his immortal ballad in his restrained, muffled, monotone, resigned, tragic voice."

Southern Suburbs

❖❖❖

LITERATORSKIE MOSTKI
30 Rasstannaya Ulitsa
(812) 166-2383
🚇 *Ligovsky Prospect*
Friday–Wednesday 11 am–5 pm (November–March),
11 am–7 pm (April–October); closed Thursdays

Blok died of his mysterious illness in August 1921. He was buried in Literatorskiye Mostki, the elite cemetery that is also the resting place of the writers Ivan Turgenev, Ivan Goncharov, and Mikhail Saltykov-Schedrin, and the literary critic Vissarion Belinsky. The official cause of Blok's death was listed as "inanition," the inability to breathe, and the vagueness of the diagnosis contributed to the popular sense that he had willed his own death out of despair. His funeral was attended by well-known writers—including Anna Akhmatova—and ordinary Russians. For most of them, Blok's death symbolized the end of the freedom and sense of possibility that they had briefly felt after the revolution.

Literatorskiye Mostki remained prestigious in Soviet times, when professors, scientists, dancers, actors, and theater directors were buried there. The large, quiet, leafy cemetery feels more like a park than a graveyard. It is unofficially divided by profession, with members of the performing arts tending to be clustered in one area and writers in another. Some of the graves can be hard to find even with the help of the English-language map on display, and it may take some looking to find the black obelisk that marks Blok's gravesite.

Andrei Bely, 1905

ANDREI BELY
1880–1934

ANDREI BELY NEVER LIVED IN ST. PETERSBURG, BUT HE IS THE AU-thor of one of the strangest and best novels to be set in the northern capital. *Petersburg* takes place over nine days in October 1905, an eventful month in St. Peters-burg's history, when strikes and protests convulsed the city and forced Nicholas II to grant the country a constitution. "Everyone feared something, hoped for something, poured into the streets, gathered in crowds, and again dispersed."

The agitation that ringed Petersburg then began penetrating even to the very center of Petersburg. It first seized the islands, then crossed Liteiny and Nikolaevsky Bridges. On Nevsky Prospect...there was a sharp drop in the percentage of passing top hats. Now were heard the disturbing anti-government cries of street urchins running at full tilt form the railway station to the Admiralty waving gutter rags.

But while Bely goes to great lengths to get the historical events exactly right, down to the soggy weather, his book is not so much about Petersburg or the 1905 revolution as it is about terror itself, for which Petersburg in 1905 turns out to be the perfect backdrop and metaphor. "Amazement and horror at life" is how one writer described the great theme of all of Bely's writing.

Bely was born in Moscow to parents who fought over everything, including him, and the chaos of his upbringing haunted Bely into his adult life. He was nervous and paranoid. He fell in love with Alexander

Palace Square with the Alexander Column

Blok's wife and pursued her shamelessly, squandering the poet's friendship. Though he never lived in Petersburg he was deeply involved—as poet, novelist, and critic—in literary circles in Petersburg and Moscow, and he happened to be in Petersburg during both the 1905 and 1917 revolutions. The writing of *Petersburg* straddled the 1917 revolution: he published the first edition to great acclaim in 1916, then rewrote much of it and issued a new version to even greater acclaim in 1922.

The principle characters are a conservative senator, Apollon Apollonovich Ableukhov ("with a stony face resembling a paperweight"), and his bumbling, philosophy-reading, lovesick son Nikolai Apollonovich, who has been recruited by leftist terrorists to blow up their most hated conservative government official: his own father. The characters wander the streets as if in slow motion, weighed down by a sense of dread, yet the story hurtles on with almost unbearable suspense.

The Ableukhovs live on the posh Angleiskaya Naberezhnaya (English Embankment) and from their mansion they look across the Neva at less grand neighborhoods: Vasilievsky Island and the Petrograd side of the city, "where the foggy, many-chimneyed distances were so wanly etched." Throughout the book the archipelago of modest island neighborhoods beyond the Neva seems always to be "cowering" or looking back at Apollon Apollonovich "in fright." His son dreads the assignment that he's somehow bungled into. Like several of Dostoevsky's heroes, he stands dazed on the city's bridges, looking into the "germ-infested" waters of the Neva, wondering how he got into this mess. Nikolai's recruiter, a student radical, is kept awake by insomniac hallucinations of cockroaches on his walls. Sofia Petrovna Likhutina, the object of Nikolai's obsessive love, is a fashionable, vaguely bohemian young woman who collects money from her rich society visitors for a "charity fund" and gives it to the students planning to assassinate Nikolai's father. The people and places of the city seem to be part of a single organism working toward its own destruction. Bely makes jabs at some of the intellectual fashions of his day, and he regularly refers to and parodies scenes from other works of Russian literature: *The Brothers Karamozov*, *Anna Karenina*, the writings of his symbolist contemporaries and of Russian and Western philosophers, which Bely studied at Moscow University.

The characters in *Petersburg* wander past the city's most majestic sights: the Winter Canal, the Troitsky Bridge, St. Isaac's Cathedral, the Admiralty, and the Summer Garden. Apollon Apollonovich, along with other ineffectual senators and political advisers ("the little old men" who "guided the movement of our wheel of state"), makes regular appearances on the grand stair-case at the tsar's Winter Palace (now the flagship building of the Hermitage Museum on Palace Square). As in Pushkin's "The Bronze Horseman" and Gogol's Petersburg tales, the city's grand landmarks and streets seem vaguely menacing. The spire of the Peter and Paul Cathedral, the Dutch-style church located within the Peter and Paul Fortress, is "pitiless" and "torment-ingly sharp." Apollon Apollonovich works in the senate, in front of which "the octogenarian doorman dozed over The Stock Exchange Register. Thus he had dozed the day before yesterday and yesterday. Thus he had been sleeping for the past five years. Thus he would sleep on."

Other scenes unfold in shabby tenements on Vasilievsky Island, mansions on the Fontanka, and other settings all around the city. Nearly every page has a reference to a Petersburg street or monument, a chal-lenge for the literary traveler.

Yevgeny Zamiatin, 1932

YEVGENY ZAMYATIN
1884–1937

$\mathcal{I}$N THE WEST, YEVGENY ZAMYATIN IS
CELEBRATED FOR HIS COMIC DYSTO-
pian novel *We*, the inspiration for Aldous Huxley's
Brave New World and George Orwell's *1984*. In Russia, however, he is barely known at all. His work was
banned under Stalin, and he was not rehabilitated until after the fall of the Soviet Union. *We*, written in
1921, depicts a conformist, atheist, perfectly rational
and efficient society of the future. Everything one
does—meals, holidays, sex—is organized according to
a master schedule, and everyone lives in transparent
glass houses watched by secret-police-like Guardians

and worships a godlike Leader. The main character is a mathematician who's perfectly at home in this world until he develops irrational feelings for a woman who seems to live according to other, "ancient," values. Zamyatin's target was not only the utopian visions of Soviet Communists but the philistinism and conformism that plagued all industrialized countries regardless of ideology. Zamyatin lived in England during World War I and was much influenced by British utopian writers like H. G. Wells. He also read George Bernard Shaw and other leftist writers critical of self-satisfied middle class culture. Zamyatin's first novel, *Islanders*, published in 1908, is set not in Russia but in the West: it's a satire about an efficiency-obsessed Englishman who had worked out a daily timetable for the entire population much like the one in *We*.

Zamyatin had been a member of the Bolshevik party for years before the 1917 revolution. He was sent to prison for participating in the failed 1905 revolution. In 1917 he welcomed the Bolsheviks' coup and eagerly returned to Petrograd from England to witness the aftermath. Like other avant-garde writers of the time, he was quickly disappointed by the mandatory political correctness that set in almost as soon as the party gained power. In 1921 he published a much-discussed article called "I Am Afraid," in which he wrote that the Soviets were harming literature by stifling writers who wrote honestly and inventively about the world around them. Writers, he wrote elsewhere, could never be "trustworthy functionaries." This article did not win him friends in the Writers Union; he was arrested later that year and briefly put in solitary confinement. He was not able to publish for the rest of his time in Russia, though *We* and other works circulated informally among writers. His story "The Cave" is a harrowing account of a Petrograd couple, Martin and Masha, living through a miserable winter soon after the revolution. They barricade themselves into one room of their apartment for warmth, a room whose contents consists of "Martin Martinych's desk, books, stone-age cakes of ceramic appearance, Scriabin opus 74, a flatiron, five potatoes lovingly scrubbed white, nickel-plated bedsprings, an ax, a chiffonier, firewood." But this firewood runs out, and by the end of the story Martin and Masha are arguing over who gets to take the single dose of poison that they've been storing in case they have to commit suicide.

Through the 1920s Zamyatin also held lectures on literature and writing from his studio in the House of the Arts, inspiring some of Petersburg's most gifted younger writers. After pleading with Stalin, he was allowed to leave the country in 1931 and moved to Paris.

SITES
Historic Center

FORMER HOUSE OF THE ARTS
15 Nevsky Prospect (at the corner of the Moika River)
🚇 *Nevsky Prospect/Gostiny Dvor*

Many artists and writers of the early 1900s came from comfortable backgrounds and were not used to having to support themselves. In the lean years immediately after the revolution, a good number of them might have starved if a few high-powered Bolsheviks hadn't stepped into help. Most important was the writer Maxim Gorky, a longtime revolutionary who had Lenin's ear even though he was openly critical of the regime. In 1919 Gorky used his influence with Lenin to organize the House of Arts, a residential community for artists and writers in a mansion on Nevsky Prospect. Admission was selective, and only the city's most promising artists and writers were given housing. Zamyatin was one of them. Though they still lived in what would seem, by today's Western standards, dire conditions, with little food and rags for clothing, residents held concerts, debates, lectures, and meetings. The mood was boisterous. As Gorky hoped, the close association of all these artists spurred their creativity. Zamyatin developed a following among some of the younger writers there, including Mikhail Zoshchenko, who would become extremely popular for his satires. Because the building looked like the prow of a ship when lit at night, and because of the raucousness and mad genius of its inhabitants, the House of Arts was known as the Crazy Ship. The huge building has recently had a facelift and now houses some of the fanciest shops and hotels in the city.

Anna Akhmatova, 1922

ANNA AKHMATOVA
1886–1966

WENTIETH-CENTURY ST. PETERSBURG IS ANNA AKHMATOVA'S CITY. SHE READ her poems at the cabarets of "prodigal pre-war days," went hungry in the post-revolutionary chaos, mourned an ex-husband executed by the Bolsheviks, and waited in line at Kresty Prison to deliver letters and packages to her son, arrested in Stalin's purges. She spent part of the German blockade in Leningrad, delivering radio addresses to galvanize the city. When the war was over she fell out of official favor again, was placed her under house arrest and constant police surveillance, and finally exiled from the city she loved. Her poetry is a testament to the suffering of all Russians during these years, but particularly those in Petersburg.

She was born Anna Gorenko in 1886 in Ukraine to aristocratic parents and grew up in Tsarskoe Selo, the town near Petersburg where the tsars had their summer palaces. Early on she felt she was destined

to be famous: as a child she told her scandalized mother that there would one day be a memorial plaque dedicated to her on their dacha in Ukraine (which turned out to be true). She wrote her first poem when she was eleven. The pseudonym "Akhmatova" came some years later: her father asked her not to publish poetry under

Anna Akhmatova with her son and her mother-in-law

their name, afraid that it would bring shame to the family. Akhmatova married the poet Nikolai Gumilev in 1910. She didn't much like him, but she felt, as she did about many things, that their marriage was a matter of fate. It was also a way for her to get out into the world. Gumilev was a published poet who lived in Petersburg and knew other writers there—he could introduce her to the capital's literary scene.

Both she and Gumilev were regularly unfaithful. Traveling in Paris in 1911, Akhmatova befriended the artist Amedeo Modigliani and probably had an affair with him. Other lovers followed. After their son, Lev, was born in 1912, Akhmatova and Gumilev arranged to have an open marriage.

Akhmatova's poetry was intimate and autobiographical. Most of her early poems were about love, or, more precisely, about love affairs that had ended. The fact of a woman poet writing frankly, in the first person, about love and desire with such artistry was unprecedented, and even more unusual was the unsentimental, clearheaded way in which she wrote about romantic affairs.

From the beginning she drew inspiration from the cityscape. The narrator of her poem "Verses about St. Petersburg" recalls the scenes of a stormy affair that has since ended; the affair is "immortal," she says, because of its association in her memory with certain landmarks of the city, "because we stood side by side/ At the blessed moment of miracles,/When above the Summer Garden,/The pink moon was resurrected."

She neither welcomed nor denounced the revolution but was apprehensive about the new order. She stayed in Russia, however, even during the horrible years between 1917 and 1921, when supplies to Petersburg were virtually cut off by the civil war and industrial mismanagement. "But not for anything would we exchange our splendid/city of glory and misfortune,/ The glistening ice of broad rivers,/The sunless, gloomy gardens/And the barely audible voice of the Muse."

Her remarkable recollections of the period describe a ghost town. "The old Petersburg signboards were still in place, but behind them there was nothing but dust, darkness, and yawning emptiness." There was no electricity or sewage disposal, and water supply was disrupted—not to speak of food deliveries. Thousands of residents were forced to leave for the countryside, where there was at least more to eat. Those who remained in Petrograd stayed indoors, and the city reverted to a semi-wild state. "You could pick a large bouquet of wildflowers in Gostinny Dvor," she wrote of the once-luxurious shopping arcade.

In the midst of this misery, Akhmatova began an affair with the man who would be her second husband, Vladimir Shileiko, a scholar of Babylonia who knew Akhmatova from her poetry readings at the Stray Dog cabaret (see below). The marriage was not happy. Shileiko was jealous of her writing, and, later, jealous of the affairs she was having with other men. They separated in 1921. Akhmatova found time to have affairs with two other men before she took up with

Nikolai Punin, an art historian who also knew her from the Stray Dog. Both Punin and Akhmatova continued to see other people during their relationship, and they never formally married, but it was the most intense and passionate attachment of their lives.

Material conditions in Petersburg improved in the early 1920s, but for Akhmatova and other non-Bolshevik intellectuals, life became worse. Gumilev was arrested in 1921 for having told someone that he would join an uprising against the Soviets if there ever were such a thing. The statement was hypothetical, but he was nevertheless executed by firing squad a few weeks after his arrest. Though long estranged, he and Akhmatova were still friendly, and she was devastated by his murder. As his former wife, Akhmatova was no longer allowed to publish her poems. Her single meager source of income was cut off, making her wholly dependent on Punin, who had his own family to support. Like the tsars, Soviet leaders had a remarkably personal relationship with the country's best writers. Stalin kept himself informed of everything that Akhmatova did and wrote.

In the next decade Stalin's Terror—which fell disproportionately hard on the residents of Leningrad—began in earnest. Massive waves of arrests and executions took place in Leningrad from 1934 until the start of World War II, when Stalin was forced to focus his murderous energies on a different enemy. About forty thousand people from Leningrad were executed, and tens of thousands of others were sent to labor camps, where many of them died under brutal conditions. Stalin's arrests first targeted the upper ranks of the Communist Party and the old Bolshevik revolutionaries but quickly widened to include people who happened to work in intellectual or elite occupations: academics, journalists, engineers, and many others. And at the height of the purges anyone at all might be arrested. "That was when the ones who smiled/Were the dead, glad to be at rest./And like a useless appendage, Leningrad/Swung from its prisons," Akhmatova wrote in *Requiem*, her cycle of poems about the Terror. The scope of the purges and the horror inflicted on the population is difficult to imagine. Akhmatova's own losses were immense. Her son was arrested three times and sent to work at the notorious White Sea Canal, the most wretched of the gulags. Punin was also arrested several times and finally died at a labor camp in 1953. The poet Osip Mandelstam, who had become one of Akhmatova's closest friends, was arrested, tortured, exiled, and arrested again before dying on his way to a labor camp.

These were the common experiences of the age, and Akhmatova would bear witness to them in *Requiem*, about a woman who waits in lines at the prison for word of the fate of her arrested son, and *Poem Without a Hero*, another cycle of poems that recalls episodes from her life in Petersburg from the cabarets of the pre-revolutionary era to the bombed-out ruins of the 1940s. She had to compose these poems mostly in secret, fearing even to write them down because the papers could be confiscated by the police. Instead, she memorized the poems and asked a few friends to memorize them as well—which had to be done silently because her apartment was bugged. Lydia Chukovskaya, a novelist and friend of Akhmatova's, recalls how the poet used to give her verses to memorize:

> Suddenly, in mid-conversation, she would fall silent and, signaling to me with her eyes at the ceiling and walls, she would get a scrap of paper and a pencil; then she would loudly say something very mundane: "Would you like some tea?" or "You're very tanned," then she would cover the scrap in hurried handwriting and pass it to me. I would read the poems and, having memorized them, would hand them back to her in silence. "How early autumn came this year," [she] would say loudly and, striking a match, would burn the paper over an ashtray.

Akhmatova's fortune changed briefly during the war, when Stalin released many political prisoners and asked popular writers, artists, and musicians to help spur the war effort. Akhmatova worked shifts as a lookout (warning residents of approaching German planes) during the siege of Leningrad in 1941 and helped to cover the statues in the Summer Garden to protect them from German bombs. Like other prominent figures, she was evacuated from Leningrad a few months into the siege and taken to the Central Asian city of Tashkent for the duration of the war. She remained in official favor for several years but was then denounced again after receiving an all-night visit from the future historian and philosopher Isaiah Berlin, then a young staff member from the British embassy in Moscow. Berlin, who was born in Latvia and knew Russian, was an admirer of Akhmatova's work even before he met her. She, in turn, was charmed by him. She told him about her experiences during the war and Terror, he told her news of her friends who had emigrated from Russia to the West. Whether there was an overtly romantic element to the visit is not clear, but Berlin declared himself to a friend to be "in love," and Akhmatova too spoke about the intensity of their meeting. Stalin did not look kindly on this visit, and Akhmatova was soon being accused in the press of sabotage. Her long-suffering son was arrested yet again, her pension was revoked, and another period of poverty and misery set in until Stalin's death in 1953 and the period of liberalization known as the thaw.

In the last years of her life a writers' organization collected money to buy Akhmatova a small country house in appreciation of her work and forbearance under the Soviet regime. Young poets made regular pilgrimages to the house, and she befriended a small group of them, including Joseph Brodsky, one of her favorites. In these years she also received hundreds of grateful letters from readers around the country who were at last allowed to admire her work openly.

THE STRAY DOG
5 Ploschad Isskustv
(also called Mikhailovskaya Ploschad)
🚇 *Nevsky Prospect/Gostiny Dvor*

Inspired by what they'd seen of bohemian Paris, Petersburg's own bohemians of the 1910s gravitated from private salons to bars, cafes, and cabarets. The Stray Dog became a favorite meeting place for all kinds of performers, including dancers, musicians, and, of course, poets. The club was named for the misfit artists—the "stray dogs"—who could find a home there. It had a stage and a piano and many small dinner tables for guests. Akhmatova, Gumilev, and Mandelstam read their poems here. Blok refused to go—by this time he was shunning the amusements of Petersburg's literary circles—but his wife read his poems there. The cabaret was free for performers, but its bourgeois guests—derisively called "the pharmacists" by the Stray Dog's owner—had to pay a cover charge. With its glamorous entertainers and reputation for decadence, the Stray Dog drew many rich business people were willing to pay the high price to see the bohemians in person. It was even visited by musicians and artists from abroad, such as the American composer Arnold Schoenberg and the Italian Futurist Filippo Marinetti.

An overpriced restaurant called the Stray Dog still exists in the old cellar location on Mikhailovskaya Ploschad, trading on its storied past to fleece "pharmacist" foreign tourists.

On Feburary 25, 1917, when a citywide general strike and bread riot paralyzed Petersburg and eventually led to the abdication of the tsar, Akhmatova happened to be in the center of town at the dressmaker's. In the afternoon she tried to get a car to take her back to her apartment on the Vyborg side of the city, but the driver refused. The neighborhoods on the Vyborg side were home to many of the city's factory workers, most of them socialists, and they were particularly restive that day.

Later in the evening, she and many other Petersburg writers and artists (including the future film director Sergei Eisenstein) went to see a performance of Mikhail Lermonotov's play *Masquerade* staged by the brilliant director Vsevolod Meyerhold at the Alexandrinsky Theater. This performance of the play—"the last spectacle of Tsarist Russia" as it was later called—became legendary for its unlikely circumstances and the devil-may-care atmosphere of the audience and actors. Most of them had to walk to the theater because there was no public transportation. In the evening the streets were deserted and mostly silent, apart from occasional gunshots. The audience filed into the theater past the dead body of a student who had been shot during one of the revolutionary skirmishes. On stage, the performers were re-creating a now-vanished imperial Petersburg. *Masquerade*, a satire of aristocratic Petersburg, is set at a fancy masquerade ball, and the stage was resplendent with gilt furnishings and lavish ball gowns and old-style military uniforms. Back outside after the play, Akhmatova heard more gunshots on Nevsky Prospect. "Horsemen with bared swords attacked passersby," she later wrote, while "machine guns were set up on the roof tops."

Vyborg Side

KRESTY PRISON
7 Arsenalnaya Naberezhnaya
(812) 542-6861
🚇 *Ploschad Lenina*
Tours Saturday and Sunday at noon, 1:30 pm, and 3 pm

Akhmatova's son, Lev Gumilev, was sentenced to be executed in 1939 and sent here to await his death. While he was held here Akhmatova would stand in line with hundreds of other wives and mothers who did not even know whether their family members were still alive and hoped to learn something of their condition or to deliver food parcels and letters. The prison wardens played cruel games with these women, promising to deliver their packages to prisoners who they knew had already been executed. Lev's sentence was commuted to five years in a Siberian gulag, but not before Akhmatova had spent seventeen months waiting in these prison lines. In her preface to *Requiem* she described an encounter with a woman who recognized Akhmatova as the famous poet:

> Standing behind [me] was a young woman, with lips blue from the cold.... Now she started out of the torpor common to us all and asked me in a whisper (everyone whispered there), "Can you describe this?" And I said, "I can." Then something like a smile passed fleetingly over what had once been her face."

Today Kresty is still a working jail. Though meant for a maximum of about three thousand prisoners, it now holds about ten thousand, all of them still waiting for a trial (sometimes for years). In 1999 the prison, bizarrely, opened its doors to tourists, who lined up for blocks to look inside this legendary place of misery. Guided tours show the prison chapel, museum, and prisoner holding area.

BIG HOUSE
4 Liteiny Prospect

🚇 *Chernyshevskaya*

This appropriately ugly building, the Petersburg headquarters of the secret police, is known to everyone as
Bolshoi Dom, or the Big House. It was built in the
early 1930s, just in time for secret police to interrogate
and torture about a quarter of the city's population
here between 1934 and 1939, including Akhmatova's
son, Lev Gumilev, and her lover Nikolai Punin. The
building stands, ironically, on the site of a former tsarist courthouse where revolutionaries, including Lenin's
brother, were tried and sentenced to death. The building is now occupied by the Federal Security Service
(FSB), the post-Communist version of the KGB.

FOUNTAIN HOUSE MUSEUM
34 Naberezhnaya Fontanka
(entrance at 53 Liteiny Prospect)
(812) 272-5895

🚇 *Mayakovskaya*

Tuesday–Sunday 10 am–5:30 pm
closed Monday and the last Wednesday of each month

Akhmatova spent thirty years of her life in a cramped
wing of the Sheremetev Palace, known to Petersburgers as the Fountain House because of its location on the
Fontanka ("little fountain") River.

The eighteenth-century building had been the
sumptuous residence of the Sheremetevs, an old aristocratic family, before the revolution. The Soviets
divided the palace into tiny communal apartments.
Akhmatova first lived here with her second husband,
Vladimir Shileiko, just after the revolution in a small
room where books overflowed from the single book-
shelf onto the floor. Like most Petersburgers they lived
in a state of semi-starvation, with Akhmatova waiting

in lines for rations and chopping trees and inessential furniture into firewood.

She moved back into the building at the end of 1926 to be with her lover Nikolai Punin, a poet and art historian who coincidentally also had rooms in the building. As hard as it is to imagine today, Akhmatova and Punin had to share the apartment, which had only a few small rooms, with Punin's wife and young daughter, who continued to live there for the next thirty years. Akhmatova's teenage son, Lev Gumilev, later joined them, as did a housekeeper with a young son of her own; still more family members came and went during Akhmatova's time there. When she and Putin ended their relationship she simply moved out of their shared bedroom into the room next door. Such were the housing shortages of the time.

It was in this apartment that Akhmatova wrote *Poem Without a Hero* and began working on *Requiem*. Lev Gumilev and Punin were arrested in the apartment in 1935 (Gumilev was arrested again in 1938 and 1949 and served a total of fifteen years in the gulags; Punin was also arrested again in 1949 and died in one of the camps in 1953). It was also here that Akhmatova spent the first few months of the war. In 1946 she was briefly placed under house arrest for her anti-Soviet views. She was made to stay in the apartment at all times and once a day had to come to the window so that a secret police agent stationed in the yard could confirm that she was alive and housebound.

Today her wing of the palace has been converted into a museum. The rooms have been arranged more or less as they were during Akhmatova's time, with many of the original objects, decorations, and pieces of furniture. Texts are available in English as well as Russian explaining how each room was used. There are also displays documenting the persecution of the intelligentsia during Stalin's reign; one glass case contains a letter that Akhmatova wrote to Stalin in 1935 pleading with him to drop the charges against her son.

Southern Suburbs

THE AKHMATOVA AND THE SILVER AGE MUSEUM
67/4 Prospect Stachek
(812) 185-0442
🚇 *Avtovo*
Monday–Friday 10–6 pm, Saturday 10 am–4 pm
closed Sunday

The unlikely setting of this museum is the neighborhood of Avtovo, one of the southern working-class sections of Petersburg dominated by high-rise apartment buildings. The museum—eight newly renovated rooms painted in jewel tones—is in one of these unassuming buildings. The Silver Age refers roughly to the poetry that emerged between the 1890s and the revolution (the Golden Age is Pushkin's). Alexander Blok, Anna Akhmatova, Osip Mandelstam, Marina Tsvetaeva, and Boris Pasternak, among others, are all associated with the Silver Age, though this museum focuses mainly on Akhmatova. She had no relationship to the neighborhood, and the museum has only a few items that actually belonged to Akhmatova (a shawl, some pieces of furniture, a lamp). The rest of the displays consist of photographs, passages from her poetry, and biographical sketches of her and other poets of the prerevolutionary generation. The museum feels like a giant shrine, and here more than at the Fountain House Museum does one feel the cultish following that Akhmatova has drawn in St. Petersburg. The texts are only in Russian.

LEV GUMILEV APARTMENT MUSEUM
1/15 Kolomenskaya Ulitsa
(812) 117-0952
🚇 *Vladimirskaya/Dostoevskaya*
Wednesday–Sunday 11 am–7 pm
closed Monday and Tuesday

Lev Gumilev, Akhmatova's son, was a historian and

poet. After he died in 1992, his last apartment, where he and his wife lived the final two years of his life, was turned into a museum. The two-room suite is relatively spacious by Soviet standards; after a lifetime spent in communal apartments, Gumilev was finally allowed to move into a decent place of his own. Everyone in the family had by then been rehabilitated politically, and Gumilev was being published both at home and abroad.

The museum is not in itself remarkable except for the fact that it still feels like an inhabited apartment, perhaps because the museum staff has a coffee pot brewing in the kitchen. The dark lacquered furniture, colorful wallpaper, watercolor paintings (many done by Gumilev's wife), and painted wooden knickknacks make the apartment an excellent example of a typical late-Soviet dwelling.

Osip Mandelstam

OSIP
MANDELSTAM
1891–1938

ONE OF THE MOST BRILLIANT RUSSIAN
POETS OF ANY AGE, OSIP MANDELS-
tam died in 1938 on his way to a prison camp where
he had been sentenced to hard labor. Arrested twice,
interrogated, tortured, and sent into internal exile on
the steppe, he was a victim of Stalin's Great Terror, in
which about five million Russians died. Mandelstam's
so-called crime was to have criticized Stalin in a poem,
calling Stalin, among other things, a "peasant slayer."
The poem was, in a sense, among the least important
of Mandelstam's creations, but it became the pretext
for his demise.

The career that ended in such darkness had a charmed beginning: when he was eighteen, Mandelstam's mother, to his embarrassment, dragged him to the editorial offices of the prestigious literary journal *Apollon* to show its editor some of her son's poems. The Mandelstams were a middle-class Jewish family from Warsaw who had moved to Petersburg so that their sons, Osip and his brother, Evgeny, could have the best possible education. Mandelstam had recently graduated from the prestigious Tenishev School (where Vladimir Nabokov matriculated some ten years later) and was planning to study at St. Petersburg University. He certainly wasn't expecting what happened next at the *Apollon* office: the editor loved Mandelstam's poems so much that he agreed on the spot to publish his work in the journal. Encouraged by his early success, Mandelstam eventually dropped his university studies to devote himself entirely to writing.

While other avant-garde poets of the era wanted to "throw Pushkin, Dostoevsky, Tolstoy, etc., overboard from the steamer of modernity," as Vladimir Mayakovksy's Futurist manifesto put it, Mandelstam considered himself an heir to the great traditions of Russian and European literature. His poems are dense with mythological, literary, and historical references, as well as contemporary allusions and tactile details: the myth of Persephone, the sacking of medieval Novgorod, and the fur coat of his friend and fellow poet Marina Tsvetaeva all find their way into his stanzas. His poems mourn lost civilizations—ancient Greece, renaissance Italy—and anticipate the eclipse of his own.

> What I am saying at this moment is not being
>   said by me
> But is dug from the ground like grains of
>   petrified wheat.
> Some on their coins depict lions,
> Others a head;
> Various tablets of gold, brass and bronze
> Lie with equal honor in the earth.

The century, trying to bite through them, left
  its teeth-marks there.
Time clips me like a coin,
And there's no longer enough of me left for
  myself.

Like most writers of his generation, Mandelstam had
been a supporter of socialism in its more humane forms,
and in the early years after the revolution he had some
hope that life would improve for Russians under the
Communists. Certainly Petersburg cultural life was
freer from government oversight than it ever had been:
no tsar, no censors, and as of yet no murderous secret
police. Any artist who could survive the crushing poverty was pretty much free to do whatever he wanted.
Mandelstam moved into the House of the Arts (p. 77),
a building set aside by the new government to house
Petersburg's artists and writers. It soon developed a
reputation as a raucous place where its half-starved yet
high-spirited residents held concerts, gave lectures, and
argued over books, art, and politics at all hours.

Still, the misery of postrevolutionary Petersburg
finally drove Mandelstam to leave the city altogether.
He went to Ukraine, where food and decent quarters
were easier to come by and where he met his future
wife. In her remarkable memoir of their life together,
Hope Against Hope, Nadezhda Mandelstam writes that
the 1920s were the most difficult years of Mandelstam's life—worse even than his later period of internal
exile—because of his disillusionment with the new Soviet society. The secret police began to harass writers,
the proletarian unions took control of cultural life, and
Mandelstam himself was falsely accused of plagiarism
by some of these Party functionaries for a collection of
translations he had edited. These accusations and the
political intrigue surrounding them were so agoniz-
ing for Mandelstam that he stopped writing poetry for
about five years in the second half of the decade.

Thousands of ordinary Soviets were recruited as
secret police informants, and Mandelstam, like every-

one else, knew that he was bound to cross paths with informants in literary circles. But even under such dangerous conditions he could not entirely disguise his views of the Soviet regime. As his widow recalls in *Hope Against Hope*, Mandelstam was unable to be dishonest; he was a terrible liar and dissembler.

In 1933 he wrote the poem about Stalin and read it to a small group of friends. One of them informed the secret police. Mandelstam was arrested in 1934 and interrogated and tortured at the Moscow secret police headquarters in Lubyanka. Stalin spared his life, in part thanks to the intervention of the poet and novelist Boris Pasternak, a friend of Mandelstam's. It was an unexpected reprieve for a writer who had directly criticized Stalin. Ordinary Russians were already being executed for smaller infractions (or for no reason at all). Instead, he was sentenced to exile for three years in the provincial city of Voronezh. He and his wife were not allowed to work, and they lived on donations from friends. After the period of exile was over they were not given permission to live in Moscow and had to keep moving from one small town to another. Mandelstam, incredibly, continued to write poetry in spite of failing health (he had two heart attacks) and emotional instability (he was profoundly disturbed by his stay in Lubyanka and tried to commit suicide shortly after being released). "My time is still unbounded./And I have accompanied the rapture of the universe/As muted organ pipes/Accompany a woman's voice." In 1938 he was rearrested and this time sentenced to hard labor in Siberia, where prisoners were routinely malnourished and worked to death. He died in transit to the east, officially of a heart attack.

SITES
Kolomna

SITE OF MANDELSTAM'S FIRST RESIDENCE
17 Ulitsa Dekabristov
🚇 *Sennaya Ploschad/Sadovaya*

"In Jewish apartments there reigns a melancholy and bewhiskered silence," writes Mandelstam in his story "The Egyptian Stamp." "It is composed of the conversations between the pendulum and the bread crumbs on the checkered table cloth and the silver glass holders." The first of the Mandelstams' own "Jewish apartments" in Petersburg was at this address, above a flower shop. Not many of the Empire's Jews were given permission to live in Petersburg, and it was, presumably, either his father's eminent position in the merchants' guild or his skills in persuasion that allowed the Mandelstams to do so. Their household was secular but inflected with Jewish traditions and concerns (he had the impression as a boy that grown-up men thought of nothing but the Dreyfus affair). In *The Noise of Time*, a series of autobiographical sketches, Mandelstam describes his father's study, with its "Turkish divan completely overwhelmed with ledgers, whose pages of flimsy paper were covered over with the minuscule gothic hand of German commercial correspondence," and "the webbed kidskins thrown about the floor, and the pudgy chamois skins with excrescences like living fingers—all this, plus the bourgeois writing table with its little marble calendar, swims in a tobacco haze and is seasoned with the smells of tanned leather."

Kolomna, the neighborhood where they lived, was a modest neighborhood of merchants, artisans, and bohemians (the poet Alexander Blok would later live nearby, and the proximity to the Mariinsky Theater meant that it was attractive to the poorer ranks of performers and musicians). The neighborhood is still relatively modest, compared to the unaffordably glitzy area around Nevsky Prospect. Kolomna's buildings are beautiful but shabby, stained with soot, their paint peeling and balconies crumbling, but prices have been going up too, and a hundred years after the Mandelstams lived here the neighborhood is becoming popular with a new wave of bohemians. Though there are tourist attractions in Kolomna, including the Mariinsky Theater and the Choral Synagogue, it's easy to wander onto streets that are untouristed and startlingly quiet, especially in the evenings.

LETNIY SAD
(Summer Garden)
*Naberezhnaya Kutuzova between Sadovaya Ulitsa
and Naberezhnaya Fontanka*
🚊 *Nevsky Prospect/Gostiny Dvor*

This lovely park, designed in the eighteenth century, has tree-lined alleys, marble sculptures of allegorical figures, and a famous, delicate wrought-iron railing separating it from the Neva. In Mandelstam's day the entry requirements were fierce: "The entrances to the Summer Garden—both the one near the river, where the railing and the chapel are located, and the one across from the Engineers' Palace—were guarded by cavalry sergeant majors bedecked with medals. They determined whether a person was suitably dressed. Men in Russian boots they drove away, nor would they admit persons in caps or in the attire of the lower middle class."

Mandelstam also recalls that the "manners of the children in the Summer Garden were extremely ceremonious. After a whispered consultation with a governess or nurse, some bare-legged child would approach the park bench and, after a bow or curtsey, would pipe, 'Little girl (or little boy—such was the official form of address), would you not like to play "London Bridge" or "Hide and Seek"?'

After such a beginning, you can imagine how merry the game was."

Today's children are much less formal (and more likely to be accompanied by a grandmother than a nanny). Young lovers and out-of-town visitors stroll the alleys in all weather, though the park is especially beautiful under snow.

NOVAYA GOLANDIYA
(New Holland)
Corner of Konnogvardeysky Bulvar and Ulitsa Truda
🚇 *Sennaya Ploschad/Sadovaya*

Mandelstam recalls in his memoir how he and his nurse would take afternoon walks through "Dutch Petersburg," the neighborhood around New Holland that was used for Naval training exercises. "Here on the roadway over which no vehicles ever passed, the marine guards held their drills, the brass kettledrums and the drums shook the waters of the quiet canal. I liked the physical selection of the men—they were taller than the normal height—and my nurse completely shared my tastes. Thus we selected one sailor, the 'black mustache' as we called him, came regularly to look at him personally, and, when we had picked him out of the formation, would not take our eyes off him till the end of the exercises."

Parts of New Holland are abandoned, but farther down Admiralteisky Canal there is a working wharf, and parts of the Pryazhka are semi-industrial.

CHORAL SYNAGOGUE AND
JEWISH QUARTER
2 Lermontovsky Prospect
(812) 713-8186
🚇 *Sennaya Ploschad/Sadovaya*
Services Saturday 10 am

His family was not particularly observant, but Mandelstam was taken at least "once or twice" in his childhood to the synagogue, which, "with its conical caps and onion domes loses itself like some elegant exotic fig tree amongst the shabby buildings." Though Petersburg never had a very well-defined Jewish quarter, the area around the synagogue did have a large number of Jewish residents. "There on Torgovaya street one sees Jewish shop signs with pictures of a bull and a cow, women with an abundance of false hair showing under their kerchiefs, and, mincing along in overcoats reaching down to the ground, old men full of experience and philoprogeneity."

Vladimir Mayakovsky, c. 1930

VLADIMIR MAYAKOVSKY
1893–1930

LADIMIR MAYAKOVSKY WAS DRAWN TO REVOLUTIONARY POLITICS WHILE still a child—it was by far the most interesting thing to do in the Georgian village where he was born, the son of a poor forest ranger from a noble family that had lost its money. When he was twelve he stole his father's guns and gave them to the local wing of Social Democratic party. At fifteen he moved to Moscow, joined the Bolsheviks, and was soon arrested for his work recruiting new members. During the eleven months that he spent in prison he read the great works of Russian and Western literature and decided he wanted to be either a poet or an artist himself.

He had no reverence for the old masters ("how easy to write better than they!") but wanted to create a new kind of art for the new era that socialist revolutionaries would soon realize. He enrolled in art school and joined the Futurists, the most radical of Moscow's many avant-garde literary and artistic circles of the early 1900s. He claimed, in fact, that Russian Futurism began the night that he and artist David Burlyuk walked out of a Rachmaninoff concert from boredom and went on to talk about other artistic disappointments: "From Rachmaninoff boredom to school boredom, from school boredom to a whole range of classical boredom." Mayakovksy made fun of genteel poets rhapsodic over "a little flower under dew." His own metaphors tend toward the violent and pungent. "Thoughts, sick and coagulated/clots of blood, crawled from my skull." He himself is "a simple man,/coughed up by the consumptive night on the dirty hand/of the Presnya." (The Presnya is the working-class Moscow neighborhood where he lived.) His love is "bright as a consumptive's flush." He promises to cherish his lover's body like a war amputee cherishes his "last remaining leg." His rhymes ingeniously put to use street slang and made-up words, his rhythms are terse and percussive. ("Maria—give!," goes a line from his poem "A Cloud in Pants.") His poems, about love and revolution, were written almost exclusively in the first person. They were detailed and confessional, dramatic, and utterly self-absorbed—qualities that would prove antithetical to Soviet values once his longed-for revolution came about.

Tickets quickly sold out for the 1913 "Futurist Festival" at the Luna Park theater in Petrograd (in a building that no longer exists but stood on the site that is now 39 Ulitsa Dekabristov), one of Mayakovsky's first appearances in the city. He played the lead role, that of the Poet, in his play *Vladimir Mayakovsky: A Tragedy*. He stood on a pedestal on stage and was visited by several maimed or suffering characters, such as "an old man with dry black cats," a man missing an eye and a leg, and a man with no head. These people tell the poet about the things they've seen and bring the poet their tears, which he collects in a suitcase. The whimsical, surreal play was not to the taste of many in the theater (some of them said that the modernist cityscape painted on the stage sets was the best part), but Mayakovsky never minded offending an audience. Like other Futurists, he would create a spectacle by walking the streets in bizarre outfits, with his face painted to depict a landscape, reciting his poetry at full volume. And he loved disrupting solemn occasions and shocking middle-class sensibilities. The writer Ivan Bunin recalls a banquet for Finnish artists in Petrograd at which the foreign minister's speech was interrupted when Mayakovsky "jumped on a chair and shouted something so obscene that [the foreign minister] was completely flabbergasted." Soon "pandemonium broke out. Mayakovsky supporters also began to yell, pounding their feet on the floor and their fists on the tables. They screamed with laughter, whined, squeaked, snorted."

Maykovsky moved to Petrograd in 1915, mainly because his new love, Lily Brik, had recently moved to the capital with her husband, the critic and publisher Osip Brik. Mayakovsky courted Lily assiduously, and they eventually began an affair that she did not hide from her husband. "I quite understand you," Osip said. "How is it possible to refuse Mayakovsky?" Their relationship was played out in public through Mayakovsky's poems, many of which were dedicated to Lily or mentioned her by name, usually excoriating her for rejecting him or cheating on him—which she did, but he too had other lovers. The affair lasted about five years (though Mayakovsky moved back to Moscow in 1918), but he was still berating Lily in letters and poems through the late 1920s, by which time he had fallen for the other great love of his life, eighteen-year-old Tatiana Yakovleva, a White Russian émigré living in Paris whom he met in his travels abroad.

He supported the Bolsheviks well into the 1920s—

it seemed he had a stronger stomach for violence than most of his fellow writers, who had by then become disillusioned and disgusted by the brutality of the new regime. The state put him to use: he wrote propaganda slogans, public service announcements promoting literacy and hygiene, and advertisements for state-owned companies. Unlike, for instance, Evgeny Zamyatin, another writer and Bolshevik party member who felt that art should never be at the service of a state, Mayakovsky saw a fluidity between art and advertising and propaganda in the new society. He genuinely tried to reconcile his art with the new political correctness, stifling as much as he could his urge to write about his own love affairs and other personal matters that had no place in a collective society. He founded LEF (Left Front of Literature), a Futurist organization for revolutionary art. LEF's magazine published some of the best literature of the 1920s, including Isaac Babel's *Red Cavalry*.

But literary life was increasingly dominated by the Association of Proletarian Writers, who supported only Socialist Realism, a conservative, sentimental, strictly representational and politically correct style that epitomized everything that Mayakovsky had always hated in art. It was depressing. He wrote two satires about Soviet philistines, *The Bedbug* and *Banya*. Tatiana Yakovleva refused to come live with him. He committed suicide on April 14, 1930, an act he'd been contemplating for years—the ultimate cure for his chronic boredom, and now for his disillusionment with the revolution that seemed to be a failure. If he had not committed suicide he would likely have been arrested, tortured, and executed in the 1930s, the fate shared by Babel, Vsevolod Meyerhold, who directed *The Bedbug*, and so many other intellectuals and 1917-era revolutionaries. A few years after Mayakovsky's death Stalin deemed him a national hero ("Indifference to his memory and to his work is a crime"), streets and metro stations were named after him, and his poetry was taught to schoolchildren.

SITES
Liteiny

—※◎※—

MAYAKOVSKY'S FORMER RESIDENCE
52 Ulitsa Mayakovskovo
🚇 Mayakovskaya

Mayakovsky found this apartment in Petersburg suitably close to that of Lily and Osip Brik, who lived at 7 Ulitsa Zhukovskovo. Osip Brik was Mayakovsky's publisher and agent, Lily the object of his romantic obsession. Mayakovsky was over six feet tall, bold-featured, and charismatic. For all that he wrote about being spurned, he had dozens of love affairs with women who swooned over him. But he was drawn to the ones who weren't so easily had. The poet had met the Briks earlier that year. At tea at their house, he launched into an impromptu recital of his poem "A Cloud in Pants." He then sat down at the table by Lily and asked if he could dedicate the poem to her. Both Briks were dazzled. Osip offered to publish the poem himself.

Vladimir Mayakovsky with Lily Brik, 1926

Mikhail Zoshchenko, 1923

MIKHAIL
ZOSHCHENKO
1894–1958

𝒜 BRILLIANT SATIRIST OF POST-REVO-
LUTIONARY LIFE, MIKHAIL ZOSH-
chenko was one of the most widely read writers of his
generation, and his work is still enormously popular
with Russian readers. Beginning in the 1920s he wrote
satirical sketches of Soviet city life, many of them set
in Leningrad and most of them involving the daily
humiliations that the working stiff endured in the
new society, and his touching and clumsy attempts
to rationalize them. Theft, long lines, corrupt bosses,
sadistic bureaucrats, overcrowded trams, and above all
poverty are commonplace in his stories, as they were

in Soviet life (he lifted some of his comic situations straight from newspaper accounts). "In breweries they pay the workers two bottles of beer each to keep them in good health," begins the story "What Generosity." But it turns out that these bottles contain a "special kind of beer—rejects. In this special beer you can find wood chips, hair, flies, bits of filth and other incredible items." The family of Ivan Gusev eagerly awaits his return from the brewery each evening with the two bottles in his pocket.

> "What's floating in it today?" Gusev's son
>   Petka asks excitedly....
> "That looks like something," said Gusev.
> "There it is!" shouted Petka, delighted. "A fly!"
> "That's right," said Gusev. "A fly. And there's
>   something else floating there, apart from
>   the fly. Is it a twig?"
> "Just a bit of stick," said his wife, disappointed.
> "Yes, it's a stick," Gusev confirmed. "But what's
>   that? It's not a cork is it?"
> His wife walked away from the table, indignant.
> "It's never anything useful round the house,"
>   she said angrily. "A bit of stick, a cork, a
>   fly. If only it was a cheap thimble, or at least
>   a button. I could do with some buttons..."
> "I want a trumpet," Petka started whining. "I
>   want a trumpet in the bottle..."

Zoshchenko was a master of skaz, a style that parodied the new official language of the Bolsheviks and the bumbling attempts of ordinary Russians to incorporate Soviet-speak into their conversation. "Citizen dog," a policeman confesses to his sniffer-dog in the story "A Dogged Sense of Smell," "I...receive three ten-rouble notes for your food and take two for myself." These stories were loved by dissidents and émigrés who enjoyed Zoshchenko's skewering of Soviet society, but they were also popular with readers who didn't read much other serious literature—the kind of simple

Soviet citizens that Zoshchenko depicted in his stories. They did not see anything mean-spirited in his humor; on the contrary, they detected a deep sympathy on Zoshchenko's part with his hapless, abused characters. Zoshchenko thought of himself as writing in the tradition of Gogol, with a strong moral dimension in his comic situations.

Born in Ukraine, he attended a gymnasium in Petersburg and studied law at St. Petersburg University. He fought in World War I and suffered debilitating pain for the rest of his life because of damage to his heart and his liver from mustard gas. After the revolution he lived in the House of Arts (p. 77), a sort of literary dormitory organized by the writer Maxim Gorky to keep the city's artists from starving to death during the years immediately after the revolution. At the House of Arts, Zoshchenko and like-minded fellows formed a literary group called the Serapion Brothers. The group did not have a distinct sensibility or ideology, though many of its members were experimenting with different forms of satire. They were united by their passionate opposition to using literature for political purposes. This of course put them squarely at odds with the new regime, and most of the writers were later punished for it. Relatively speaking, Zoshchenko got off easy.

His great popularity in the 1920s and 1930s helped him survive Stalin's Terror. He was not arrested during the Terror like most of Leningrad's intelligentsia. His popularity was so great that it probably gave even Stalin pause. After World War II, however, when Stalin was reviving his campaign against the intelligentsia, Zoshchenko (along with Anna Akhmatova) was attacked viciously in *Pravda* and forbidden to publish his work. The pretext for this denunciation was a children's story that Zoshchenko had written about a monkey who escapes from his cage at the zoo. The monkey spends the day studying Soviet humans in their natural habitat and decides he'd rather go back to the zoo. Zoshchenko's income was nearly cut off, and among his jittery fellow citizens he became a pariah: everyone was afraid of being arrested for associating with him. Though he outlived Stalin, Zoshchenko was still forbidden to publish under Khrushchev, and he died in poverty without having been pardoned. His stories were published again in the 1960s, their classic Soviet predicaments and black humor no less relevant to the new generation of readers.

SITES
Historic Center

━━━━━✦◉✦━━━━━

ZOSHCHENKO FLAT-MUSEUM
4/2 Malaya Konyushennaya Ulitsa, No. 119
(812) 315-2773
🚇 *Nevsky Prospect/Gostiny Dvor*
Tuesday–Sunday 10:30 am–6 pm; closed Monday and the last Wednesday of each month

The museum is in the two-room apartment where Zoshchenko lived for the last three and a half years of his life, from January 1955 to July 1958. The building was a co-op for the Leningrad department of the Writers Union and full of other writers and journalists. Today it's an ordinary residential building, somewhat the worse for wear, and visitors walk through a typical St. Petersburg courtyard and ring a bell at the door as if they were visiting a friend. One room of the museum contains a small exhibition hall with old editions of Zoshchenko's books, political posters, and newspaper articles (including the article in *Pravda* denouncing him), and a chronology of his life (in Russian). The other room is furnished just as the Zoshchenkos kept it, with their own furniture and actual items that belonged to the writer, including his typewriter, a pair of shoes, and a suit jacket. Zoshchenko's son was convinced that there would one day be a museum dedicated to his father, and he carefully kept his father's belongings and his library (some seventeen hundred volumes) intact for the future Zoshchenko museum.

Vladimir Nabokov and his father, 1906

VLADIMIR
NABOKOV
1899–1977

$\mathcal{A}$N INTERRUPTED ST. PETERSBURG
CHILDHOOD LIES IN THE DISTANT
past of many of Vladimir Nabokov's characters—émigré writers, biographers, and professors who are separated by time and geography and political circumstance
from the prerevolutionary city they remember. Nabokov himself lived in Petersburg only from his birth in
1899 until his family fled the Bolsheviks in 1917. Even
this eighteen-year span is misleading—the Nabokovs
spent all of their summers at their rural estate and
many of the winters at European resorts. In his memoir, *Speak Memory*, the country birch forests and for-

eign beaches loom larger than Bolshaya Morskaya, the fashionable Petersburg street where his family had a mansion. Nabokov never returned to his native city after the revolution. If he had, he might have felt like the narrator of his novel *Look at the Harlequins*, an exile who visits Leningrad one summer in the 1960s expecting a rush of memories, only to realize that the vernal city is totally unfamiliar to him—he had never spent a single June or July day of his childhood there.

Yet the family house in St. Petersburg was, according to Nabokov, his only real home in the world. The

The Nabokovs' house in St. Petersburg

Nabokov family had a long history in the capital: they had served the tsars in military and civil service from at least the time of Peter the Great. Both of his parents had family fortunes, and his father, a passionate advocate of liberal reform, was deeply involved in politics and civic affairs. When Tsar Nicholas II finally allowed for a parliament in 1906, the elder Nabokov was elected to it. He was well known in the city, caricatured in the newspapers by his political adversaries, and highly respected by most everyone else. He also liked to live well: he kept a staff of fifty servants and sent his shirts to England for laundering.

Nabokov *fils* did not inherit his father's interest in politics. In *Speak, Memory* he doesn't dwell on the horrors of the revolutionary years. He was the oldest and favorite child, doted on by his parents. He and his four siblings had a succession of foreign nannies and private tutors who taught them English and French as well as Russian. The few outright mentions of violence in his memoir are startling for their measured tone and the contrast with his otherwise contented childhood. Nabokov grew up between two revolutions—the failed one of 1905 and the disastrously effective one of 1917—whose skirmishes took place on his neighborhood streets. In some linden trees a few blocks from his house, "an ear and a finger had been found one day— remnants of a terrorist whose hand had slipped while he was arranging a lethal parcel in his room on the other side of the square. Those same trees…had also seen children shot down at random from the branches into which they had climbed in a vain attempt to escape the mounted gendarmes who were quelling the First Revolution." His mother had been so frightened by the shooting of children near their house that she moved the family to a different apartment for two years. During those same two years, Nabokov's father served three months in prison for urging Russians to resist the tsar. Years later, from a window in his mother's room, the teenaged Nabokov watched some of the early battles of the 1917 revolution and saw a dead body for the first time, being carried away on a stretcher by fellow fighters ("an ill-shod comrade kept trying to pull off the boot" from one of the dead man's legs).

Fearing for the safety of his family after the Bolshevik coup, the elder Nabokov sent them to the Crimea, which was not yet Red, and later joined them there. Lenin's army pressed south, and in spring of 1919 the Nabokov family fled for Europe. Nabokov found himself, along with his younger brother, a charity case at Cambridge University while the rest of the family settled into a shabby Berlin exile, in "one of those large, gloomy, eminently bourgeois apartments that I have let to so many émigré families in my novels and short stories." Three years later his father was killed while trying to shield his friend from an assassin.

Nabokov began writing seriously when he graduated from Cambridge and moved to Berlin, quickly developing a reputation in the émigré communities of Berlin and Paris as the most talented Russian writer of his generation. In Berlin Nabokov jealously guarded his Russian language, fearing that it might be corrupted the longer he lived abroad. He disdained the idea—so important to latter-nineteenth-century Russian novelists—that fiction should convey philosophical or political or religious ideas. (He particularly scorned Dostoevsky's "vulgar soapbox eloquence" and "completely pathological idealization of the simple Russian folk.") He stayed in Germany until 1937—far longer than was probably prudent, given that had married a Jewish woman, fellow Petersburg exile Vera Slonim. They fled the Nazis for Paris.

He was, effectively, two different writers: the young émigré who wrote ten novels in Russian had a quiet death in Paris, where the second writer, the one who worked in English, took over. He wrote his first English novel, *The Real Life of Sebastian Knight*, while living in France. He had it with him as a calling card when he washed up on US shores in 1940, again keeping only a step ahead of the Nazis. In order to write novels and stories in English, Nabokov felt that had to give up Russian prose entirely (though he continued to write poetry in Russian). In his second language he produced *Lolita*, *Pnin*, and *Pale Fire*, among other books. He described the experience as "like learning anew to handle things after losing seven or eight fingers after an explosion." With the success of *Lolita*, published in 1955, he no longer had to rely on teaching for extra income, and in 1961 he and his wife left the United States. for Montreux, Switzerland, where he lived and wrote until his death in 1977. Nabokov never returned to the Soviet Union, but his sister did so regularly after 1969 and Nabokov used her observations of Soviet life in *Look at the Harlequins*.

SITES
Historic Center

NABOKOV MUSEUM
47 Bolshaya Mosrkaya Ulitsa
(812) 315-4713
🚇 *Sennaya Ploschad/Sadovaya*
Tuesday–Friday 11am–6 pm, Saturday–Sunday
12 pm–7 pm; closed Monday

The Nabokovs' mansion at 47 Bolshaya Morskaya had luxuries barely heard of in most of Russia: five bathrooms, electric lights, an elevator, and, in the garage, a Benz (in an era when most Petersburg residents traveled by horse-drawn carriage or sleigh). Like all private property, the mansion was claimed by the government after the revolution. Some of the rooms became a newspaper bureau. The director of Leningrad's *banyas* (public bathhouses) had his office in Mrs. Nabokov's boudoir. Another part of the house became a censor's office—ironic, given the fate of Nabokov's books in the Soviet Union.

While private businesses took over most of the building after perestroika, a few rooms on the first floor were opened as a museum in 1998. Visitors walk by the marble staircase in the entrance hall, under which the Nabokovs' doorman used to sharpen dozens of pencils for the political meetings that were held in the house. This doorman turned out to be a double agent of sorts: he was recruited by the tsar to report on Nabokov senior's political activity. In 1917 he also led Bolshevik agents to the safe where the Nabokovs kept their family jewelry, which the agents promptly seized in the name of the proletariat. But Nabokov emphasizes that "the nostalgia I have been cherishing all these years is a hypertrophied sense of lost childhood, not sorrow for lost banknotes."

Museum guests can also see the dining room, green drawing room (so called for the color of its walls), and library of the house, where Nabokov's father would practice fencing and boxing every morning with the children's French fencing instructor. "I would dash, with my fur coat half on, through the green drawing room (where an odor of fir, hot wax and tangerines would linger long after Christmas had gone), toward the library, from which came a medley of stamping and scraping sounds. There, I would find my father, a big, robust man, looking still bigger in his white training suit, thrusting and parrying, while his agile instructor added brisk exclamations ('*Battez!* '*Rompez!*') to the clink-clink of the foils."

Almost none of the Nabokovs' furniture or belongings have survived, though the museum is slowly acquiring some of Vladimir Nabokov's personal effects. The rooms display Nabokov memorabilia, including first editions of his books in English and Russian, as well as his Scrabble board, donated by his son. The museum also hosts readings and concerts and an annual Bloomsday celebration on June 16.

FORMER TENISHEV SCHOOL
44 Mokhovaya Ulitsa
🚇 *Nevsky Prospect/Gostiny Dvor*

When Nabokov was eleven his parents sent him to a private Petersburg boys' school known for its progressive ideals. Given the democratic ethos of the Tenishev School, Nabokov's arrival there every morning in a chauffeured Benz, his use of French phrases, and his complete disinterest in politics did not endear him to his teachers, who accused him of showing off. ("I don't like him. He's a loner with no sense of community spirit," reported one of his teachers.) Even more extravagantly, Nabokov paid out of his own pocket to publish a book of his poems at age seventeen. His Russian literature teacher, whom he greatly admired, mortified him by devoting an entire class to a critique of the book (the criticisms, Nabokov admits, were well deserved).

WHOLE TOUR OF THE CITY COULD BE PLANNED AROUND THE PLACES where the young Nabokov and his first girlfriend, Valentina Shulgina, used to meet in their desperate attempts to find some privacy. Museums were the most promising settings. "The Hermitage, St. Petersburg's Louvre, offered nice nooks, especially in a certain hall on the ground floor, among cabinets with scarabs, behind the sarcophagus of Nana, high priest of Ptah." Rooms 30 and 31 of the Russian Museum "offered a bit of privacy because of some tall stands with drawings—until a foul-mouthed veteran of the Turkish campaign threatened to call the police." They moved on to the Alexander Suvorov Museum—which honors the eighteenth-century general who led the Russians to victory in Poland, Turkey, and France—and other, more obscure museums that no longer exist. "But wherever we went, invariably, after a few visits, this or that hoary, blear-eyed, felt-soled attendant would grow sus-

Nevsky Prospect near Gostiny Dvor, 1900

picious and we would have to transfer our furtive frenzy elsewhere." They also visited Petersburg's two movie theaters, one of which, the Parisiana, still stands on Nevsky Prospect. And "when museums and movie houses failed us and the night was young, we were reduced to exploring the wilderness of the world's most gaunt and enigmatic city." They walked through the city's immense public plazas, whose windy expanses were the undoing of Akaky Akakievich in Gogol's story "The Overcoat."

In the squares, various architectural phantoms arose with silent suddenness right before us. We felt a cold thrill, generally associated not with height but with depth—with an abyss opening at one's feet—when great, monolithic pillars of polished granite (polished by slaves, repolished by the moon, and rotating smoothly in the polished vacuum of the night) zoomed above us to support the mysterious rotundities of St. Isaac's cathedral. We stopped on the brink, as it were, of these perilous massifs of stone and metal, and with linked hands, in Lilliputian awe, craned our heads to watch new colossal visions rise in our way—the ten glossy-gray atlantes of a palace portico, or a giant vase of porphyry near the iron gate of a garden, or that enormous column with a black angel on its summit that obsessed, rather than adorned, the moon-flooded Palace Square.

Daniil Kharms

DANIIL
KHARMS
1905–1942

"I AM INTERESTED ONLY IN 'NONSENSE'; ONLY IN THAT WHICH MAKES NO PRAC-tical sense," wrote Daniil Kharms, author of short sto-ries, plays, poems, and children's books. Only his chil-dren's books, plus a handful of poems, were published during Kharms's lifetime, for he had the bad luck to be an experimental writer during the worst years of Stalin's repression.

Kharms was born and lived his entire life in St. Petersburg. In the city he gained some renown as a young man not only for his poems (which he read in public and eventually published in two volumes), but also for his eccentric behavior. Like Futurist poet Mayakovsky and other avant-garde writers of the time, Kharms liked to make theater out of life. He dressed like a dandy and carried his own cutlery ("the family silver," as he would say) with him to bars and cafés, refusing to eat with any other. In the late 1920s he and some of his colleagues formed their own literary group, OBERIU, roughly an acronym for the Association of Real Art. Real art, for them, was purposely obscure, yet playful and not at all self-serious. They favored illogical statements and nonsense plots. Among their sayings were, "Art is a cupboard" and "Poems aren't pies; we aren't herring." Kharms and his colleagues wanted to turn the ordinary meanings of words on their heads in hopes of revealing some deeper truths about our relationship to the material world.

In 1928, OBERIU staged an event in Leningrad called "Three Leftist Hours," which included poetry readings, film screenings, and a performance of Kharms's play *Elizabeth Bam*, in which two men come to arrest a woman, Elizabeth Bam, for an unnamed crime. Songs and circus tricks follow, and by the end of the play Elizabeth's father has come on stage to kill one of the two men arresting her, a murder that seems to be carried out solely with words, crucial among them the refrain "Glory to the feathers!"

As the 1920s waned, the climate for avant garde writers became hostile, and Kharms supported himself by writing whimsical children's stories full of clever rhymes and wordplay about round-bellied samovars, cats with helium balloons, birds playing musical instruments, and other unlikely creatures. The authorities denounced OBERIU's styles as "reactionary sleight-of-hand" in 1930, and soon after Kharms was arrested (for "deflecting the people from the building of socialism by means of trans-sense verses") and exiled for a short time to the northern city of Kursk. When he was released he found it hard to get work and was desperately poor, though he was still allowed to write children's books sporadically over the next decade. He spent much of the Thirties in a state of semi-starvation ("This is how hunger begins:/The morning you wake, feeling lively/Then begins the weakness,/Then begins the boredom;/Then comes the loss/Of the power of quick reason,/Then comes the calmness/And then begins the horror."). He wrote dozens of short stories, sketches, plays, and bits of memoir, none of which would be published for another fiftysome years.

Kharms was arrested in 1941 and died in a prison hospital in 1942, most likely of starvation. Though he was posthumously rehabilitated during Khrushchev's thaw in the early 1960s, Russians weren't familiar with his short stories until decades later, when they were finally published in full. His children's books, however, were reissued in the 1960s and have remained extremely popular.

SITES
Liteiny

KHARMS'S FORMER RESIDENCE
11 Ulitsa Mayakovskovo
🚇 *Mayakovskaya*

Kharms lived and worked for years at 11 Nadezhdinskaya Ulitsa, now known as Ulitsa Mayakovskovo. In August 1941 the superintendent of the apartment building called him downstairs "for a few minutes." When he came down he was arrested, still in his bedroom slippers.

Joseph Brodsky, 1972

JOSEPH BRODSKY
1941–1996

HEN JOSEPH BRODSKY WAS ARRESTED AND TRIED IN THE WINTER OF 1963–1964 for "decadence and modernism" and "a world view damaging to the state," he had not yet had a single one of his poems published. It's a testament to the government's paranoid thoroughness that it had on its radar a twenty-three-year-old poet whose oeuvre was a stack of typewritten pages about love affairs, the passage of time, and John Donne. Even an unpublished poet couldn't count on being left alone in the Soviet Union, not if he was talented and had a brash, original voice that attracted a following in Leningrad. Until the fall of the Soviet Union, writers were enormously important both for the government—which was scared of them—and for the public, who looked to them to stand up to the regime and to express everything about life that most people didn't dare articulate. Brodsky himself lamented the pressures put on a poet in the Soviet Union—they were liable to distract him from his primary responsibility: "to write well."

Brodsky was born in Leningrad in 1941. His father was a naval officer and a reporter for the navy. His mother worked as a bookkeeper in various offices. They lived very modestly, as so many Soviet citizens did, in their communal apartment at the corner of Liteiny Prospect and Pestel Street. He was bored at school and dropped out at fifteen, an unusual move for the son of educated parents in the Soviet Union that gives a sense of his rare independence of mind. He taught himself Polish and, eventually, English, made money as a translator, and also went through a series of unlikely odd jobs, from dissecting corpses at a morgue to assisting geologists at a crystallography lab at Leningrad University. The latter led to a series of geological expeditions to Siberia and the White Sea area in Russia's far north. It was on one of these expeditions that he started reading poetry, and very soon he was writing poems himself. He couldn't publish them, not being an officially recognized poet, but he read at private gatherings, where people sometimes wrote down the poems and gave them to friends. This was before the days of organized samizdat, or self-publishing, of underground literature. Brodsky's poems were simply passed around by people who liked them. He quickly became known in Leningrad by word of mouth. "Sometimes within one city," he later recalled, "you'd walk into somebody's apartment, and he or she would show you a bundle of your work." A friend of his, the poet Evgeny Rein, introduced Brodsky to Anna Akhmatova, who often met with younger poets (known as Akhmatova's orphans) at her dacha at Komarovo. Brodsky became a favorite of hers—she gave him a volume of her work with the inscription, "To Joseph Brodsky, whose poems seem to me to be magical."

His poetry was not especially political. But he wrote about private experience and, like Osip Mandelstam, a poet he much admired, considered himself an heir to the great cultures of the West. A poem of his might refer to Greek mythology, the Bible, the English metaphysical poets. This was enough to draw the attention of Soviet authorities. Though Khrushchev had ushered in a period of liberalization immediately after Stalin's death, he became afraid of the wave of creative expression that he'd let loose. The postwar generation was listening to jazz, reading Robert Frost and William Faulkner and F. Scott Fitzgerald, and, increasingly, creating unofficial art and literature that flouted the rules of socialist realism. Brodsky was one of the first victims of the president's crackdown on the intelligentsia in the 1960s. At the end of 1963, an article appeared in a Leningrad newspaper denouncing Brodsky's "pessimistic" poems. A few weeks later, KGB agents surrounded Brodsky on the street and forced him into a waiting car. He was interrogated and charged with "parasitism"—meaning, essentially, that he was writing poetry without official permission—and held in Kresty Prison (p. 87) and two psychiatric hospitals while awaiting trial (dissidents were often confined to such hospitals, where officials tortured them under the pretext of administering treatments).

Brodsky's arrest and trial did not have the effect that Khrushchev intended. The poet had a large group of friends and admirers who attended the trial to offer moral support and secretly copied down the courtroom dialogue and circulated a transcript among the public. He had a lawyer who quickly proved that he had a legitimate job as a translator and was not involved in any of the outlandish anti-government conspiracies he was charged with. Brodsky himself was not intimidated in the courtroom. One exchange between him and the Soviet judge became legend. She asked him a series of questions about who had given him permission to be a poet and who had taught him to be one. Brodsky, of course, had a different view of literary credentials than she did. "I don't think it comes from education," he said of the ability to write poetry. "I think that it's from God."

These words electrified the public. Brodsky's courage made him a hero to many Soviet citizens, particularly the country's younger generation. He received a sentence of five years' exile and labor near the arctic city of Archangelsk, but his sentence was commuted after just eighteen months because of public pressure both within the Soviet Union and from abroad. He became a cause of the Western left; Jean-Paul Sartre wrote Khrushchev a letter arguing that his treatment of Brodsky was giving Communism a bad name. After Brodsky returned to Leningrad, a few of his poems were finally published in literary journals, and more were smuggled abroad and published in the United States. Some of them refer to his lack of freedom and the vulgarity of Soviet culture, but most are more personal and movingly capture the rhythm of Russian life.

> When it's Christmas we're all of us magi.
> At the grocers' all slipping and pushing.
> Where a tin of halvah, coffee-flavored,
> is the cause of a human assault-wave
> by a crowd heavy-laden with parcels:
> each one his own king, his own camel.

But Khrushchev's successor, Leonid Brezhnev, had a new strategy for making high-profile dissidents shut up: he sent them to the West, where they were cut off from family, friends, and their Russian audience. In 1972, Brodsky was forced to leave the country, warned that if he stayed, the upcoming winter would be a "very cold" one. The University of Michigan invited him to be a poet in residence, and so he moved to the United States, where he continued to write poetry and also taught college literature classes ("the function/to which I'd been appointed was to wear out/the patience of the ingenuous local youth"). He was never again able to see his parents—every year they applied to the Soviet government for permission to visit him, and every year they were denied.

He won the Nobel Prize in 1987, and in 1991 he was named US poet laureate, the first foreign-born poet to win the title. By this time his poetry was widely available in the USSR and he was still passionately loved by the reading public, who hoped that he would come back for a visit to read his work. But he never returned to Russia, even after the fall of the Soviet Union, when he easily could have received permission to do so.

SITES
Liteiny
—❧◉❧—

BRODSKY'S FORMER RESIDENCE
24 Liteiny Prospect
🚊 *Chernyshevskaya*

Brodsky describes his family's apartment in a haunting essay about his parents and Leningrad childhood called "In a Room and a Half." The essay's title refers to the tiny living space that he and his parents shared during his childhood and adolescence. The "half" is a small alcove where Brodsky himself slept, divided from the main room (where his parents slept and where all three of them did their living) "by two large, nearly-ceiling-high arches which I constantly tried to fill with various combinations of bookshelves and suitcases in order to separate myself from my parents."

Theirs was a communal apartment, meaning that the six rooms of the original "bourgeois" apartment were split up—under the supervision of the Soviet housing bureaucracy—among different families, who all shared the same kitchen and bathroom. Their communal apartment had relatively few residents, as only eleven people shared their bathroom and kitchen, compared with dozens in other communal apartments.

What barbs or medical and culinary advice, what tips about goods suddenly available in this or that store are traded in the communal kitchen in the evening when the wives cook their meals!...What silent dramas unfurl there when somebody is all of a sudden not on speaking terms with someone else!...What depths of emotion can be conveyed by a stiff, resentful vertebra or by a frozen profile! What smells, aromas, and odors float in the air around a hundred-watt yellow tear hanging on a plait-like tangled electric cord. There is something tribal about this dimly lit cave, something primordial—evolutionary, if you will; and the pots and pans hang over the gas stoves like would-be tom-toms.

This way of living was common in Soviet days, especially in the old city center, where aristocratic mansions and middle-class apartment buildings were split up after the revolution. In the 1950s rings of huge new apartment buildings started going up around the city's core (each decade bringing taller and uglier buildings, culminating in the signature poured-concrete Soviet bloc high-rise of the 1970s), but until then most of the city's residents were crowded into older communal apartments.

The street where the Brodskys lived was, in pre-revolutionary times, one of the most fashionable and upscale parts of the city, and also a center of literary activity. By coincidence, the Brodskys' communal apartment in a building called the Muruzi house, was the same one in which the poet Zinaida Gippius and scholar Dmitri Merezhkovsky lived and held their famous weekly salon. From the balcony of the Brodskys' room Gippius had "shouted abuse to the revolutionary sailors" in the streets, Brodsky writes.

BRODSKY EXHIBIT
FOUNTAIN HOUSE MUSEUM
34 Naberezhnaya Fontanka
(entrance at 53 Liteiny Prospect)
(812) 272-5895
🚇 *Mayakovskaya*
Tuesday–Sunday 10 am–5:30 pm; closed Monday and
the last Wednesday of each month

The apartment where the Brodskys lived is still a private home and thus not open to the public as of this writing. There are plans under way to establish a Brodsky museum in the Muruzi house, but in the meantime there's a room dedicated to him in the Anna Akhmatova museum at the Fountain House (p. 88). The Brodsky room contains much of the contents of his study in South Hadley, Massachusetts, where he lived and taught at Mount Holyoke College until his death in 1996. There's a desk with W. H. Auden's picture on it, a small collection of books (*Journals of Stephen Spender*, *Globe Illustrated Shakespeare*), a typewriter, a quilt. Across the windows the curators have put translucent screens with a projection of the actual view from Brodsky's South Hadley House. Upon request, the museum guide can play a recording of Brodsky reading some of his poems.

Vasilievsky Island

NAVY MUSEUM
4 Birzhevaya Ploschad
(812) 328-2501
🚇 *Vasileostrovskaya*
Wednesday–Sunday 10:30 am–4:45 pm; closed Monday,
Tuesday, and the last Thursday of each month

Brodsky calls this museum, formerly the stock exchange, the most beautiful building in the city. After the war Brodsky's father, a naval officer, was in charge of the photography department at the museum.

"On late afternoons, school over, I'd wade through the town to the river, cross the Palace Bridge, and run to the museum to pick up my father and walk home with him.... 'Greetings, Commander,' I would say, for such was his rank; he'd smirk back, and as his tour of duty wouldn't be over for another hour or so, he'd cut me loose to loiter about the museum alone."

The museum contains, as it did in Brodsky's childhood days, paintings, model ships, tools, and other artifacts of the Russian navy, including the sailboat that Peter the Great took out on the waters every day. The emperor loved sailing and the sea (one of the reasons he moved the capital from landlocked Moscow to Petersburg), and he effectively created the Russian navy from scratch, having studied the most sophisticated shipbuilding techniques of the seventeenth century in Holland.

> There is hardly anything that I've liked in my life more than those clean-shaven admirals, en face and in profile, in their gilded frames looming through a forest of masts on ship models that aspired to life size. In their eighteenth- and nineteenth-century uniforms, with those jabots or high-standing collars, burdock-like fringe epaulets, wigs and chest-crossing broad blue ribbons, they looked very much the instruments of a perfect, abstract ideal, no less precise than bronze-rimmed astrolabes, compasses, binnacles, and sextants glittering all about. They could compute one's place under the stars with a smaller margin of error than their masters! And one could only wish they ruled human waves as well: to be exposed to the rigors of their trigonometry rather than to a shoddy planimetry of ideologues.

Around 1950, during a wave of anti-Semitism orchestrated by Stalin, the Politburo decreed that

Jews could not hold high rank in the military (or many other desirable jobs). Brodsky's father was decommissioned and forced to leave his job at the museum. He eventually found work as a photojournalist for a newspaper run by the St. Petersburg branch of the Merchant Marines.

Kolomna

NOVOYA GOLANDIYA
(New Holland)
Corner of Konnogvardeysky Bulvar and Ulitsa Truda
🚇 *Sennaya Ploschad/Sadovaya*

Not long before he died, Brodsky was asked by Russian television interviewers what his first stop would be if he were to return to St. Petersburg. His answer was Novaya Golandiya. This triangular island of crumbling red brick buildings, bordered by the Admiralteisky and Kryukov canals, was a shipbuilding center in the 18th century, named for the country whose shipbuilding accomplishments stirred the naval ambitions of Peter the Great. It continued to be a navy depot through the twentieth century, sinking into disrepair during the late Soviet years. The old warehouses, surrounded by thick trees, overgrown grass, and far more greenery than is seen on most Petersburg blocks, have an eerie charm. The street along the narrow Admiralteisky Canal is especially picturesque, with the canal and brick industrial buildings on one side, and a row of apartment houses pressed close to the street on the other. The area is most beautiful at twilight, when cats prowl near the water and the neighborhood's human inhabitants are strolling home from work. But Novaya Golandiya will not remain a peaceful oasis for long: British architect Norman Foster and Russian real estate magnates are said to be planning to build luxury hotels and an outdoor amphitheater on the island.

SELECTED BIBLIOGRAPHY

Billington, James H. *The Icon and the Axe: An Interpretive History of Russian Culture.* New York: Vintage, 1966.

Binyon, T. J. *Pushkin: A Biography.* New York: Knopf, 2003.

Brown, Edward J. *Russian Literature Since the Revolution.* New York: Collier, 1963.

Clark, Katerina. *Petersburg: Crucible of Cultural Revolution.* Cambridge: Harvard University Press, 1995.

Feinstein, Elaine. *Anna of All the Russias: A Life of Anna Akhmatova.* New York: Knopf, 2006.

Figes, Orlando. *Natasha's Dance: A Cultural History of Russia.* New York: Metropolitan, 2002.

Frank, Joseph. *Dostoevsky: The Seeds of Revolt, 1849.* Princeton: Princeton University Press, 1976. *Dostoevsky: The Years of Ordeal, 1850–1859.* Princeton: Princeton University Press, 1983. *Dostoevsky: The Stir of Liberation, 1860–1865.* Princeton: Princeton University Press, 1986. *Dostoevsky: The Miraculous Years, 1865–1871.* Princeton: Princeton University Press, 1995. *Dostoevsky: The Mantel of the Prophet, 1871–1881.* Princeton: Princeton University Press, 2002.

George, Arthur L., and Elena George. *St. Petersburg: Russia's Window to the Future—The First Three Centuries.* Lanham: Taylor Trade, 2003.

Mandelstam, Nadezhda. *Hope Against Hope: A Memoir.* New York: Scribner, 1970.

Mirsky, D. S., Prince. *A History of Russian Literature.* New York: Knopf, 1949.

Nabokov, Vladimir. *Nikolai Gogol.* New York: New Directions, 1944.

LIST OF ILLUSTRATIONS

ACKNOWLEDGEMENTS

For their guidance and generosity the author is grateful to Nadia Aguiar and Angela Hederman at The Little Bookroom; Eda, Ilya, and Leonid Maizles and Esther Verokhovskaya in St. Petersburg; Dina and Robert Blair; and Aaron Matz.

ABOUT THE AUTHOR

Elaine Blair was born in St. Petersburg and now lives in New York, where she is on the staff of *The New York Review of Books*. Her essays and reviews have appeared in *The New York Review of Books*, *The American Scholar*, *The Nation*, and *The Village Voice*.